EssentialJESUS

EssentialJESUS

100 readings through the Bible's greatest story

for individuals and small groups

Whitney T Kuniholm
President, Scripture Union USA

EssentialJESUS

Published in the UK by Scripture Union, 207–209 Queensway, Bletchley, MK2 2EB, England.

 Scripture Union: We are an international Christian charity working with churches in more than 130 countries providing resources to bring the good news about Jesus Christ to children, young people and families – and to encourage them to develop spiritually through the Bible and prayer. As well as coordinating our network of volunteers, staff and associates who run holidays, church-based events and school Christian groups, we produce a wide range of publications and support those who use our resources through training programmes.
Email: info@scriptureunion.org.uk
Internet: www.scriptureunion.org.uk

Scripture Union Australia: Locked Bag 2, Central Coast Business Centre, NSW 2252
www.su.org.au

© Copyright Whitney T Kuniholm 2007

ISBN 978 1 84427 238 9

Cover design by ie Design of Birmingham, UK.

Internal design and typesetting by Creative Pages: www.creativepages.co.uk.

Printed and bound in Great Britain by Creative Print and Design, Ebbw Vale, Wales.

CONTENTS

Meet the author of EssentialJESUS

Whitney T Kuniholm lives in Exton, Pennsylvania. He and his wife Carol attend an Episcopal church where Whitney is involved in prayer ministry, two small fellowship groups for men and occasional teaching and preaching. Carol is the Director of Ministry to Youth and their families at the church and son-in-law Steve is the worship leader there so, as Whitney says, the challenge at family get-togethers is to talk about something other than church! As well as their married daughter Anna, Whitney and Carol have two other children: Matthew (in the Peace Corps) and Stephanie (in college).

Whitney is the President of Scripture Union in the USA, a position he has held since 1997. In this role, he gives leadership to SU's ministry throughout the United States, which includes evangelism and discipleship programmes for children and young people, as well as the promotion of daily Bible reading and prayer among people of all ages.

Whitney has written six books, all on the subject of personal and group Bible study, including **Essential100**. He has also written articles for various newsletters and Christian magazines.

When he's not working or writing, Whitney enjoys golf, running or working out at the YMCA. He's a fan of Starbucks coffee, classical, bluegrass and jazz music, and National Public Radio. He also finds time somehow to get involved as a volunteer at an inner-city ministry for homeless women and their children. He comments, 'It constantly amazes me what a difference it makes to share the love of Christ in very basic ways to people at the absolute bottom of the ladder.'

Introducing EssentialJESUS

- *If Jesus was the most influential person in history, I'd like to learn more about him.*

- *I know people have strong opinions about Jesus, and that's fine. But I'd like to find out for myself what he said and did so I can come to my own conclusions.*

- *Of course I know who Jesus is; who doesn't? I've just never taken the time to read all that the Bible says about him.*

- *I've heard people say, 'I'm a follower of Jesus.' But what does that really mean?*

No matter what you think about Jesus, there's no denying he is the most influential person in all of human history. And what's truly amazing is that his path to influence was so unlikely.

Jesus never became a political, military or government leader; he never wanted to. He never owned a multinational corporation or acquired any wealth to speak of; he didn't need it. He never wrote a book, never staged a concert tour, never appeared on television and never had a radio chat show or even his own blog. He was born in a barn, grew up as a labourer, remained single and childless his entire life and was executed at the age of 33.

Yet somehow Jesus became the reference point for life ever since; we mark our calendars by his death. He has inspired some of the world's greatest art, literature, music and architecture. His ethical teachings have been hailed as the world's greatest – even by those who aren't his followers. He's been the subject of countless books, articles, television programmes and films. Today his Church has more members than any other religion in the world – and persecution only makes it grow larger. Not only that, the book that gives us the most information about him – the Bible – has sold more copies than any volume ever printed.

What's so special about Jesus?

That's what we hope to discover in **EssentialJESUS.** We'll take an honest look at what Jesus said and did, so we can determine who he really was and is. To do this, we'll read and reflect on 100 carefully selected passages from the Bible. And we'll approach our journey not as theological experts but as open-minded seekers who want to get a true understanding of the most influential person in history. Are you ready?

The Bible's greatest story

Many people have a basic knowledge of what the Bible is about. They know it describes how God created the world and how he has been involved with it ever since. Not only that, many have read some of the Bible's most popular stories, like the account of Adam and Eve in the Garden of Eden, perhaps Moses and the Exodus, David and Goliath, Jonah and the whale, Daniel in the lion's den, Peter on the day of Pentecost and Paul on the road to Damascus.

But the one story people seem to know the best is the story of Jesus. Every Christmas we are reminded of the familiar account of Joseph and Mary travelling to the little town of Bethlehem, of Jesus' birth in a manger and of the angels singing 'Glory to God in the highest, and on earth peace, good will toward men' (Luke 2:14, KJV). But why is that story more important than all the rest? Because, as you'll see, Jesus is the focal point of God's plan to save the world from sin and to offer people eternal life. The greatest story in the Bible is Jesus; from Genesis to Revelation the Bible is literally 'his story'.

So as we follow the storyline of Jesus through the Old and New Testaments, we'll not only get a clear understanding of the **EssentialJESUS** but also we'll get a good overview of the Bible. Here's how the 100 readings are organised.

Who is Jesus? We'll begin our journey with five readings from some contemporaries of Jesus: two of his disciples (Peter and John) and the apostle Paul, a man who had a unique encounter with Jesus soon after his resurrection. Each of these five readings gives us a soaring description of Jesus and his significance. They are some of the most inspiring and memorable passages in the Bible and together they form a sort of prologue to our exploration of the **EssentialJESUS**.

The Old Testament Our next 25 readings take us to the Old Testament, because the story of Jesus began long before the manger. In the very first book in the Bible we get our first indication that God was planning to send a Messiah, a Saviour for the world, which raises an obvious question: why do we need a saviour? Once we come to grips with the answer (hint: the answer is sin! – the wrong things we do that separate us from a perfect holy God), we'll then trace what the Bible says about this coming saviour in the Psalms and in the writings of the prophets. You'll be amazed how much the Old Testament has to say about this future saviour and how perfectly Jesus matched the picture God had been describing for centuries.

The New Testament The longest part of our journey, 65 readings in all, will follow the story about Jesus in the New Testament. We'll read the accounts of Jesus found in the four Gospels of Matthew, Mark, Luke and John. We'll examine his birth, ministry, teaching, miracles, death and resurrection, and the establishment of his Church. And we'll explore the unfinished part of his story – that is, the time in the future when Jesus will return to earth for all those who believe in him. By this point in the journey, you'll have a complete picture of the **EssentialJESUS**.

Who is Jesus to you? In the final five readings, you'll get an opportunity to do something really important: form your own opinion about Jesus. To help, we'll consider several people who came face to face with Jesus. Some rejected him; some embraced him. But, in each case, you'll see that Jesus pressed the issue. Why? Because his desire is to have a relationship with every person, including you. That was God's plan from the beginning and it's why Jesus came to earth.

My story

Before we go further, there are two things I want to clarify. First, even though I am a committed follower of Jesus Christ myself, I'm not going to force my beliefs on you. What you believe is your responsibility. What I hope to do in this book is guide you through the Bible so that you can weigh things up and come to your own conclusion about Jesus. Second, as we take this journey together, I'm also going to share some of my personal experiences and observations. I've learned that both the Bible and all of life can teach us about Jesus.

So now that you know where I'm coming from, let me tell you how my relationship with Jesus began.

I grew up in a Christian home and spent lots of time at church, Sunday school and Christian camps. I can't remember a time when I didn't know about Jesus. But I can remember the first time I consciously said 'yes' to being his follower. I was six years old and sitting in a Sunday night church service led by my father. At the end, he asked everyone to close their eyes and then said something like, 'If anyone wants to give their heart to Jesus, I want you to raise your hand right now.' I didn't really understand everything he was saying. All I knew was that I wanted to give my life to Jesus – to follow him. So I raised my hand.

By the time I got to college many years later I began to wonder, 'Do I really believe what I accepted as a child?' One thing that especially bothered me was that although I knew a lot about the Christian faith, I didn't seem to *feel* much. How could I determine if my faith was real? During that time, I went to a week-long series of evangelistic meetings. At the end, the preacher asked people to come forward and make a public commitment to follow Jesus. This created a dilemma for me. I already believed in Jesus or, at least, I thought I did. Did a Christian need to get saved?

Feeling unsure, I walked to the front, hoping that some wise person would counsel me through my question. But no one joined me at the altar rail. Everyone was busy praying with others. So I quietly whispered the shortest prayer I've ever prayed. 'Thank you, Jesus.' That's all I said before I began to cry – to really sob. It lasted for quite a while. Again, I didn't really understand what was happening, but I believe that God was letting me know that he could not only touch my mind but he could touch my heart as well. Today, whenever I take communion in church, I always whisper that prayer as I walk back to my seat. 'Thank you, Jesus.' It's my way of affirming that I'm still his follower.

That's how it happened for me. But the fact is, everyone has a different experience. Some people struggle with the decision to follow Jesus. Others come to it more easily. It's important that you find out who Jesus is and then come to your own conclusion about him. I believe it's the most vital decision you'll ever make.

Using EssentialJESUS

At this point you may be thinking, 'Hold on. I'm interested in Jesus but I can't read *the BIBLE!* It's too long and confusing.' If so, don't worry; most people feel that way. That's why I've designed this book to make your journey through the Bible easy and meaningful. Let me begin by making a few suggestions that will get you off to a good start.

First, **EssentialJESUS** is designed to be used... with a Bible! It tells you what Bible passage to read and then helps you reflect on the main points. Obviously, without reading the Bible passage, **EssentialJESUS** won't make much sense. Be sure to use a translation of the Bible that's easy for you to read. Although the King James Version (KJV) is beautiful and widely available, it is often difficult for readers today to understand, since it was translated into the language of 1611. I recommend that you use one of the many excellent modern translations such as the New International Version (NIV), New Living Translation (NLT) or the Contemporary English Version (CEV). If you are still unsure about which Bible translation to use, you might want to check with a pastor, minister or priest.

Second, **EssentialJESUS** guides you through 100 short Bible passages, all of which relate to Jesus. The readings are undated so you can complete them at any pace – over 100 days, six months, a year or more. Whatever schedule you pick, don't feel guilty if you miss a day. Trust me, you will! Just do the next reading whenever you have time and before you know it you'll make it through all 100. Also, I've grouped the readings into sets of five that begin with an introduction that alerts you to important themes. You might try to do one set of five readings each week.

Third, you will notice that for each reading I've followed a five-step format:

Pray – Read – Reflect – Apply – Pray

This is a pattern you can use any time you read the Bible. In the Bible, God speaks to you. In prayer, you can respond to him. So, by integrating the two, you can have a dialogue with God. Here are some additional ideas on how to get the most out of the five steps:

PRAY before you read, asking God to help you understand his Word (the Bible). The written prayer will get you started, but feel free to add thanksgiving, confession, praise or whatever you'd like to express to God. Remember, you're beginning a dialogue.

READ the Bible passage carefully. If you have time, you may want to read the passage more than once, or look at the surrounding passages to get an understanding of context. Keep a pencil or highlighter handy, so you can make notes or underline key phrases or verses.

REFLECT on what you've read. First, summarise your own observations on the passage in the margins or in a separate notebook. It may help to ask:

• What was the main point of this passage?

• Which verses relate to my life now?

Then think further about the passage by reading my reflections.

APPLY what God teaches you from his Word to your life. Take some time to think this through. Did the passage contain

• an example to follow?

• a warning to heed?

• a promise to claim?

How should this affect your thoughts, words and actions? You might want to jot down how you'd like to apply these things in your life.

PRAY again, asking God to help you live out his Word. This time, turn the things you've learned into prayers. Also, pray about your own needs and the needs of others. And be sure to thank God for any answers to prayer.

Don't go it alone

At the end of each section, I've included a page of discussion questions. Why? Because *the best way to use this book is to read it with another person, or as the basis of a group study experience.* Each week, try to complete a set of five readings on your own. Then, get together with your friend or group to talk about what you've learned. Start by encouraging each person to share their own insights from the readings. Then, use the discussion questions to help you continue your conversation. You'll find that reading the Bible with others creates a positive motivation to keep going and makes your experience of God's Word more meaningful.

Your higher goal: meeting God

From beginning to end, the Bible tells the story of how 'God so loved the world that he gave his one and only Son, that whoever believes in him shall not perish but have eternal life' (John 3:16). So, as you begin your journey through the greatest story in the Bible, keep in mind that your goal is not just to make it to 100 or to gain more Bible knowledge or even to develop greater spiritual discipline. Those things are important, but your higher goal is to get to know Jesus. The secret to making the Bible come alive is to view reading it as an opportunity to have an encounter with the risen Christ – the one who loves you, who died for you and who desires to have a living relationship with you.

My prayer is that, over the next few months, the Bible's greatest story will come alive for you as never before. But don't let **EssentialJESUS** be the end of your engagement with the Bible. Let this journey become the beginning of a lifetime adventure of meeting God every day in the Bible and prayer.

Whitney T Kuniholm

WHO IS JESUS?

What is the most important question in all of human history? Of course, everyone is curious about their own existence: Who am I? Where did I come from? Where am I going? In addition, many wonder about the great challenges in the world today: How can we stop war and maintain peace? How can we find a cure for cancer? How can we eliminate poverty? How can we protect the environment?

But I'm convinced there's one question more important than all the rest: Who is Jesus Christ? Is he really who he claimed to be? Jesus said he was God come to earth. That's right; he said he was God's promised Messiah, the one and only Saviour of the world – the only way to God. And if that's true – really true – then I want to suggest that everything else is secondary.

When you think about it, our world is full of information about Jesus – in movies and plays, on television and radio, and in magazines and books. Some of it is accurate, some not. Often he's positioned as the founder of a religion – Christianity. Other times he's portrayed as a moral teacher, a miracle worker or a martyr. Some see him as a revolutionary, a charlatan or a curse. There are some who don't think he existed at all; they think the stories of Jesus are legends and myths.

So how do we find out who the **EssentialJESUS** really is? The best way is to go to the most complete source of information we have about him: the Bible. As you read through the 100 passages about Jesus that I've selected, you'll quickly see that the storyline of Jesus is the 'scarlet thread' that runs through the Bible from beginning to end. Jesus is what the Bible is all about.

In our first five readings, we'll consider the thoughts of three people who were close to Jesus: John and Peter, two of his key disciples; and Paul, who had a unique encounter with Jesus. Each of these readings describes Jesus in the most amazing terms. Later in our journey, we'll get to the particulars of his life. But for now we need to get the big picture and that's where we'll start.

1

Truth beyond facts

Date:

PRAY   Dear God, I'm curious to find out who Jesus really is –
and to know for sure if that's important. Please help me
take an honest look at him.

READ   John 1:1–18

REFLECT

Journalists like to think of their profession as a quest for truth; if they
accurately report all the facts of a story then they believe they have
told the whole truth. But as John, the writer here, begins his account
of the life of Jesus, he realises that truth goes far beyond mere facts.
The man he lived alongside for three years was divine and human at
the same time. How do you describe a truth like that?

The other Gospel writers start with the practical details of Jesus' life –
who his ancestors were (Matthew), how he was born (Luke), and how
his public ministry got started (Mark). John starts by calling Jesus 'the
Word' – a curious phrase but one that captures something important:
Jesus was a statement from God to humanity. 'If you want to know
who I am, look at Jesus.' Why? Because 'the Word was God' (1:1). Not
just a great teacher or healer, celebrity or leader. The essential truth
about Jesus is that he was God on earth (1:14).

That's a pretty bold claim! But if that's true, what difference does it
make?

First, *Jesus is a new source of light in the world* (1:5–9). John uses the
image of light and darkness to describe Jesus' mission. A world
without God is a sinful, dark place. If you need proof, just turn on
your television. When Jesus appeared he was like a candle in a dark
room; people could finally see a way to God.

Second, *Jesus is the source of new life* (1:4,12). If you believe there is no
God, then there is no afterlife; death is the end. But Jesus invites
everyone to be part of God's family both now in this world and for
ever (1:12).

As we begin to explore what the Bible says about Jesus, we need to
remember that the facts tell only part of the story. The truth about
Jesus doesn't contradict the facts. It's just far, far bigger.

APPLY   Has God ever communicated with you? How? How did
you respond?

PRAY   Jesus, as I learn more about you, I'd also like to
experience more of you in my life. I ask for your help…

2   Living like Jesus

Date: *Who is Jesus?*

PRAY   Father, in the midst of my busy, stressful life... I want to be still, just for a few minutes... so I can hear from you...

READ   Philippians 2:1–11

REFLECT

During the 1960s there was a revival of interest in Jesus in the West. In a decade of radical change, he seemed like an ideal role model. Young men tried to look like him; they had long hair, grew beards and even wore leather sandals (a classmate of mine called them 'Jesus boots'). But what does it mean to live like Jesus?

In this passage Paul, who came to prominence as a leader of the early Church after a dramatic conversion, was writing to the Christians in Philippi encouraging them to be less selfish and more loving, compassionate, joyful and united (2:1–4). Good advice for Christians at any time. But the question was how? Paul's answer was simple: live like Jesus. He proceeds to give one of the most soaring descriptions of Jesus in the entire Bible (2:5–11). Let's unpack what he says:

Jesus is God (2:6). Ever since Paul had an encounter with the risen-from-the-dead Jesus (Acts 9:1–9), he fearlessly talked about his experience. Do you have such an encounter to share?

Jesus became a human being (2:7,8a). He wasn't a spiritual Caspar the Ghost. He lived with us (John 1:14). How real is Jesus to you?

Jesus humbled himself (2:7). The creator of the universe was willing to serve his creatures. Are you willing to serve those 'lower' than you?

Jesus obeyed God (2:8). For him it meant death on the cross. What does obeying God mean for you today?

Jesus was exalted by God (2:9). God brought Jesus back to life. Are you convinced that Jesus is still alive today?

Jesus will be acknowledged by everyone (2:10,11). No matter what you believe about him now, one day you'll come face to face with Jesus. What will you say when you do?

Whether it's the first century, the 1960s or today, living like Jesus begins with a decision to follow the One who 'became obedient to death – even death on a cross' (2:8). Now *that's* a radical idea.

APPLY   What is one thing you could do to serve someone close to you this week, as humbly as Jesus did?

PRAY   Imagine that you are face to face with Jesus right now. What do you want to say?

3   It's all about Jesus

Date: *Who is Jesus?*

PRAY   God, show me something new about your Son today.

READ   Colossians 1:15–23

REFLECT

For a long time, we had several cans of concentrated grape juice in our larder. It looked like standard grape juice, but if you forgot it was concentrate and tried to drink straight from the can, you'd have a hard time swallowing it.

In a way, that's what our passage today is like; it's concentrated truth about Jesus and you may have a hard time swallowing everything you read. That's okay. The reason we're covering this passage now is that in just a few verses it introduces us to several of the major themes about Jesus that we'll be exploring on our journey through the Bible.

The book of Colossians was written by Paul, a leader of the early Church, to counteract the impact some false teachers were having on the new believers in the city of Colosse. These teachers had devised complicated schemes to describe how people should relate to God. It sounded impressive but something important was missing: the glory of Jesus. Theology, teaching and our view of the Church are vital to Christian faith. But if Jesus is not at the centre, we've missed the point.

To correct the problem, Paul offers a concentrated description of Jesus that echoes some of the things we've already discovered. The main point is that Jesus is God (1:15,19; 2:9) and he's behind and in all creation (1:16,17).

Paul builds on this foundation with two new insights that add to our picture of Jesus. First, *Jesus is the head of the Church* (1:18). If you eliminate the head, the body dies. Second, *Jesus is the key to the good news* (1:20–23) – that because of him we can have a relationship with God. Without him, we are alienated from God.

Churches today are still plagued by false teaching. We would do well to follow Paul's example; he started with the positive (1:3–14), and then says, in effect, 'Let's get back to basics … it's all about Jesus.'

APPLY   In your opinion, what are the 'basics' about Jesus? Do you find any claims about him hard to swallow?

PRAY   Thank you, God, that you made a way for me to have a relationship with you and that way is Jesus.

4   What is God like?

                                                         Who is Jesus?

PRAY   Dear God, I'm hungry to know you better, thirsty to experience you more.

READ   Hebrews 1:1–4

REFLECT

I once saw a video of young children being asked the simple question, 'What is God like?' I laughed when the first adorable child looked straight into the camera, smiled and answered, 'I don't know.' The next child shrugged and said, 'Don't know.' And another: 'Don't know.' Several more gave the same answer. The last child just shook her head and looked down.

What *is* God like? No matter how old you are, that's not an easy question. But the writer of the Bible book called *Hebrews* (we don't know who it was) has the best answer. If you want to know what God is like, look at Jesus; he's the 'exact representation' of God (1:3). Want to know what God thinks about the world? Look at Jesus. Want to know what God likes and dislikes? Look at Jesus. Want to know what God thinks about people? Or about you? Look at Jesus.

Hebrews will go on to cover all kinds of issues that were important to the first Jewish Christians, as well as to us. But it starts with an important fact: God has always wanted people to know who he is and he's been saying so for centuries (1:1). But, in Jesus, God goes even further. He shows up himself and says, 'Look! *This* is who I am.'

And make no mistake: although Jesus was human, he was no ordinary guy. He's the human expression of God, who died for sins, came back to life and returned to his place in heaven (1:3). He is still present with us through the Holy Spirit. That's the gospel in a nutshell.

As we pursue the essential Jesus through the pages of the Bible, we will confront a man like no other, who is a God like no other.

APPLY   How would you describe what God is like? How could you communicate that to someone this week?

PRAY   Heavenly Father, I'm so thankful that you want me to know who you are. In spite of all my distractions, my heart's desire is to know you.

5   The big Church

Date:

Who is Jesus?

PRAY   It's so good, Father, to spend time reading and reflecting on your Word.

READ   1 Peter 2:4–10

REFLECT

Have you ever heard someone say, 'Jesus is my personal Lord and Saviour'? No doubt people who say that are sincere and want us to know of their commitment to following Jesus. But, to some, the statement sounds a little exclusive, as if the Christian faith is about 'me and Jesus and no one else'.

In our passage today, the apostle Peter opens our eyes to another important truth about Jesus: saying 'yes' to following him makes someone part of a really big group called the Church. We'll unpack this idea later in our journey (especially in the section entitled *The Early Church of Jesus*), but for now let's try to get the basic concept.

To describe the Church, Peter uses a picture of bricks and mortar, but gives it a new spiritual meaning. The Church is like a 'spiritual house' made up of Jesus ('the living Stone') and his followers ('living stones'). In other words, the Church is not a physical building; it's a 'people belonging to God' (2:9), with Jesus Christ as its foundation (2:6).

And he's not a lifeless, granite memorial from the past. Jesus is alive and present in his Church today (2:4). Those who accept him will find him a firm foundation for their lives but those who reject him will find him a stumbling block.

The church I attend is old and built of grey stone. Over the years the congregation has grown and recently we expanded the facilities. When the new building was finally complete we saw that one of the walls had been built around a large stone cross. It makes a lasting statement about what we believe: this church is built around Jesus Christ. That's exactly what the Peter is saying in this passage, only the Church he's referring to is much, much bigger.

APPLY   Are you one of the living stones in God's spiritual house? How do you know?

PRAY   Spend some time praying to experience Jesus as the foundation for your life.

DISCUSSION QUESTIONS: WHO IS JESUS?

After you've completed the five readings in this section, get together with another person or group to talk about the things you've learned. Begin by sharing the insights you gained from your own reflection on the passages. Then use the following questions to help you continue the conversation.

1   What would you say is the most common understanding about Jesus today? What does 'the average person' believe about Jesus?

2   What have you learned about Jesus from films, plays, television or novels? How is Jesus portrayed in popular culture?

3   How and when did you first learn about Jesus? Has your understanding of Jesus changed over the years? If so, how?

4   How would you describe your view of Jesus today?

5   Do you think it matters what people believe about Jesus? Why/ why not?

6   Do you think Christians should actively try to persuade other people to believe in Jesus? Why/ why not?

7   Do you think Jesus is different from any other of the world's great religious leaders? If so, how?

THE NEED FOR A SAVIOUR

The Bible teaches that Jesus is the Saviour of the world. But that raises an obvious question: Why do we need to be saved? What problem is so great that God himself had to come to earth to solve it?

In a word, the problem is sin – people missing the mark of God's standard for us – and that's the theme of our next five passages.

We'll begin by reading the account of 'the original sin', when Adam and Eve disobeyed God in the Garden of Eden. A scene featuring a talking serpent might seem comical to today's readers. But the reality of Satan and evil is not funny at all.

Next, we'll consider a classic example of how sin spreads from an individual to a community, as we read how the people of Israel worshipped a golden calf. We can only imagine how different things would have been if Aaron had responded to the request for an alternative god by saying, 'No way!' Simple though it may sound, saying 'No way' is still a good strategy for avoiding sin today.

We'll finish the section by reading a few examples of what the psalms and the prophets had to say about sin. And guess what? It's not positive! We'll come face to face with God's angry side. He really doesn't like sin at all.

Some people wonder if all the talk about sin is unnecessarily negative. Doesn't it just make us feel guilty? Who needs that? Wouldn't it be better to focus on the positive themes in the Bible, like peace and love? Not really. Sin isn't something we can avoid if we're careful, like having a bad hair day. Rather, sin is more like a congenital heart defect; we're born with it.

The good news is that Jesus came to deal with our sin problem. But before that can happen we need to understand our problem; we have to get to grips with why we need a Saviour in the first place.

6

It's sin!

Date:

The need for a Saviour

PRAY   Lord God, I'm hungry for a closer relationship with you. Enable me to sense your presence as I reflect on your Word...

READ   Genesis 3

REFLECT

I grew up as the oldest of four children. That meant I was expected to be a good influence on my siblings. Sometimes it worked out that way and sometimes... let's just say I had a different agenda! So when my mom reached boiling point with me, she'd play her ultimate trump card: 'If you do that again,' she'd say with conviction, 'it's sin!'

But what exactly is sin and where did it come from? That's the question this passage answers for us. Adam and Eve had the perfect life; no work, no worries, no problems. All they had to do was obey one simple rule and paradise was theirs for ever (2:16,17). It sounds easy, but it's not. There's something about human nature that draws us to disobey God's rules (Romans 7:7–25).

As a young child I once stomped up the stairs holding my ears, shouting back at my parents, 'If you say no, that means I *have* to do it!'

We tend to think sin is some obviously evil act, like murder or stealing and, of course, that's part of it. But the full picture is more subtle and dangerous. Note that the serpent doesn't ask Eve to reject God. He simply questions God's authority (3:1) and contradicts God's Word (3:4). Honest questions and even doubts can help us grow in our faith. But questioning God's authority and living in contradiction to what he says in the Bible is a different matter. That *is* sin.

And sin has consequences, as we see in this passage: shame (3:7), fear (3:10), pain (3:16) and death (3:19). But the worst consequence is a broken relationship with God; we're banished from his presence (23), doomed to live with an empty, God-shaped hole in our hearts and unable to re-establish a relationship with him on our own (3:24). No wonder we need a saviour.

APPLY   How would you define sin? How do you deal with it in your life?

PRAY   Heavenly Father, it's sometimes hard to admit, but it's true: I need a saviour.

7

Stupid sin

Date:

The need for a Saviour

PRAY   'Speak, LORD, for your servant is listening... ' (1 Samuel 3:9,10).

READ   Exodus 32:1 – 33:6

REFLECT

How can they be so stupid? The Israelites had witnessed God at work in guidance and provision ever since he miraculously released them from bondage in Egypt. Yet they can't wait for Moses to return with the Ten Commandments. In their impatience, they whip each other up into a frenzy of hedonism and pagan worship. It's a poignant reminder about the nature of sin. No matter how good we've been in the past, we're never immune from sin's influence in the present.

Think about Aaron. In some ways, you can't fault him; all he did was give the people what they wanted (32:1,2). That's what political leaders are supposed to do, right? The problem is, Aaron's position was that of *spiritual* leader; his actions affected the moral and religious life of the community. In a way, all of us are spiritual leaders, even if we aren't ordained. Our actions influence the moral decisions of others, for good or for ill.

In contrast, think of the influence Moses had on the people of Israel. He certainly wasn't the life and soul of the party (32:19,20,25–29). He took a strong stand against the idolatry and wild behaviour he saw all around. Today, it may seem enlightened to believe that sin 'ain't nobody's business but my own'. But the problem is, it's not true. Ultimately our sin is God's business; it's his commands that we violate (32:8) and his consequences we must pay (32:33,34). Again it highlights our need – our desperate need – for a saviour.

But even in the middle of this out-of-control situation we see a wonderful example of God's plan for dealing with our sin problem. Moses volunteers to take the punishment the people deserved (32:31,32); he was willing to make what we call 'atonement' (satisfying the requirements to restore our relationship with God: 32:30) – exactly what Jesus did on the cross thousands of years later.

APPLY   Who has been the greatest influence for good on your life? Whose life have you influenced the most?

PRAY   Dear Jesus, I can't thank you enough for what you did on the cross. Thanks for your willingness to take my punishment...

8   Not just the bad guys

Date: *The need for a Saviour*

PRAY   Father, help me understand more about the sin problem as I read your Word today.

READ   Psalm 14

REFLECT

Years ago, my wife and I made friends with a couple who didn't go to church. They were committed to their marriage, loving parents and involved in the community. But they were firm in their resistance to organised religion. Why? They said they didn't want to damage their son's self-esteem by exposing him to any talk about sin.

It would be nice if sin only affected the 'bad guys' of the world, those who deny God (14:1) and aggressively pursue an evil agenda (14:4). There's no doubt it does; we only have to read the daily newspaper to see evidence of that. But David says sin also affects the 'good guys'. We've all 'turned aside'; we're all 'corrupt'. No one is good, 'not even one' (14:3).

That may seem harsh or negative at first, especially for those who identify themselves with 'the good guys'. But if sin affects everyone, as David states, then it's not healthy to deny its hold on us. And that's why a good church is so important. Like a good hospital, it doesn't give us disease; it helps us diagnose and deal with it.

But it's important not to let our understanding of sin cause us to misunderstand God. It's true, he hates sin. But it's not true that he enjoys catching people out in their sins, as so many seem to think. In fact, his desire for us is just the opposite; he's actively looking for those who are seeking a deeper relationship with him.

David ends his psalm with a prayer for a saviour: 'Oh, that salvation … would come out to Zion!' (14:7). God answered that prayer centuries later when he sent his Son, Jesus Christ, to restore all people from captivity to sin. That's reason to rejoice and be glad!

APPLY   What picture of God do you have from this psalm? What do you want most from him?

PRAY   Dear God, help me to understand you better and experience you more.

9

He's against it

Date: *The need for a Saviour*

PRAY   Dear Lord, strengthen my relationship with you as I
              spend time reading your Word.

READ   Isaiah 59

REFLECT

US President Calvin Coolidge was famous for giving short answers.
Once questioned about a church service he had attended, he was
allegedly asked: 'Did you like the sermon today?'
Coolidge: 'Yes.'
Question: 'What was the sermon about?'
Coolidge: 'Sin.'
Question: 'So... what did the preacher say about sin?'
Coolidge: 'He's against it.'

This chapter from Isaiah reminds us once again that God is against
sin. We should be too, for several important reasons:

Sin separates us from God (59:2). We first saw this when Adam and Eve
were evicted from the Garden of Eden (Genesis 3:23,24). By the time
of Isaiah, people were even more distant from God, having lost the
ability to experience his presence and communicate with him at all
(59:2). Today, the distance has become so great that some people
mistakenly think God is dead, or that he never existed at all.

Sin leads to a breakdown of fundamental values. The modern bumper
sticker that reads 'No justice, no peace' could just as easily have been
written by Isaiah (59:8); he mentions justice six times in this chapter
alone. This is not politics. Biblical justice means doing what's right for
all people, especially the poor and oppressed (Psalm 82:3,4).

Sin causes a rejection of truth. Isaiah used the image of a person
stumbling and lost in the street (59:14,15). Most people today believe
in some form of their own truth. But when truth becomes relative,
society loses its reference points and wanders ever further from God.

It's no surprise that God is against sin. What is surprising is that in
spite of our continual rebellion against him, God had a plan to save us
from it all along (59:20,21). The plan was to send Jesus Christ – who
could restore the broken relationship for ever.

APPLY   In what ways could you demonstrate that you are
              'against' sin?

PRAY   Thank you, heavenly Father, that you've always had a
              plan for me to find forgiveness from my sin and a new
              relationship with you through Jesus.

10

Date:

Ho, ho, ho?

The need for a Saviour

PRAY   Father God, you know how busy I am in my daily life. You also know how much I need to be still and know that you are God.

READ   Amos 5

REFLECT

Do you ever wonder how God feels when we sin? Some people might think God's like a shopping mall Santa Claus. He doesn't really know what we've done, and he doesn't really care. He just chuckles and promises to give us what we want. Well, not exactly...

As we've discovered in this passage, God has some pretty strong things to say to people who go through the motions of worship without acknowledging their sin. 'I hate, I despise ... I cannot stand ... I will not accept ... I will have no regard ... I will not listen ...' (5:21–23). That's no shopping mall Santa.

We might want to be more euphemistic about sin: 'Well, nobody's perfect,' we say. Or: 'We all have our little peccadilloes.' Or: 'That's just the way I am.' But it's important not to gloss over the fact that God hates sin with a passion.

That's the message the prophet Amos had for the people of Israel in the eighth century BC. They were piously attending worship and longing for the day when God would punish everyone else – 'the day of the LORD' (5:18). But God was angry because these highly religious people weren't practising what they preached. They abused the poor in order to live in luxury (5:11); they manipulated the courts and deprived innocent people of justice (5:12). In short, society had become so corrupt that good people were afraid to speak out (5:13). Some say that Amos could be describing western society and the Church today.

It can be frightening to think of God being so angry. But only when we understand the depth of his revulsion for sin can we fully appreciate the height of his love for us in sending his own dearly loved Son. Jesus Christ willingly died to pay for the consequences of the sins of the world that God hated so much. That's not anger; it's overwhelming love.

APPLY   Amos encouraged his readers to seek the Lord (5:4,6). How could you do that this week?

PRAY   Thank you, Father, for your deep love for me which prompted you to send Jesus to deal with the consequences of my sin.

DISCUSSION QUESTIONS: THE NEED FOR A SAVIOUR

After you've completed the five readings in this section, get together with another person or group to talk about the things you've learned. Begin by sharing the insights you gained from your own reflection on the passages. Then use the following questions to help you continue the conversation.

1   How did you first become aware that there was such a thing as sin?

2   How do you define 'sin' now?

3   Do you think the Church and Christian people focus too much on sin? Or not enough?

4   How does it make you feel to know that God hates sin? How does it make you feel that God solved the sin problem himself?

5   Do you think it's fair to say God has an 'angry side'? Why/ why not?

6   When have you ever sensed a need for a Saviour in your life?

7   Do you think it's possible to understand the good news about salvation without understanding the bad news about sin? Why/ why not?

TRAILERS OF A SAVIOUR

Anyone who's ever watched television or been to the cinema knows what a trailer is. It's a short promotion for a coming attraction. Usually the trailer captures a quick taste of the most exciting parts of the full film and, by the time you've seen several, you have a pretty good idea of what's coming.

In our next five readings, we'll take a look at some fascinating trailers of coming attractions found in the Bible. These are often referred to as 'types'. A biblical 'type' is simply a person, thing or event in the Old Testament that points towards Jesus Christ in the New Testament. Many people find that a basic understanding of types or 'typology' brings a new richness to their understanding of the Old Testament.

We must be careful, however, not to overdo our search for types. Some have tried to impose deep meaning on every detail in the Old Testament and, as a result, have come to some very speculative conclusions. This may be good for selling books but it does not promote sound teaching!

Even so, there is no need to 'throw the baby out with the bathwater' since Jesus himself said that the Old Testament spoke about him (John 5:46).

To maintain our balance, we will consider five Old Testament types that are specifically referenced in the New Testament – the Passover, the manna in the wilderness, Moses lifting up the serpent, the Temple and Jonah in the great fish. As you'll see, each one of these gives us a unique picture of the Saviour who would appear centuries later.

As we launch into our study of Old Testament types, we can be encouraged that we are following a teaching method that Jesus used with the two disciples on the road to Emmaus: 'And beginning with Moses and all the Prophets, he [Jesus] explained to them what was said in all the Scriptures concerning himself' (Luke 24:27).

11

Significant symbols

Trailers of a Saviour

PRAY   Lord God, help me to understand you better as I read
             your Word today.

READ   Exodus 12:1–30

REFLECT

Our passage today may seem a little gruesome, as it involves killing
animals, handling blood and sudden death. But, in fact, this is one of
the most important passages in the Bible. The Passover represents a
dramatic breakthrough in the Old Testament as well as a symbol of the
most significant event in the New Testament. Let's step back and get
the context.

God's people, the Israelites, had been slaves in Egypt for 430 years.
The man God had chosen to rescue them, Moses, had challenged the
Egyptian leader nine times with a message from God: 'Let my people
go!', each time accompanied by a severe plague. Now God unleashes
the tenth and final plague – the death of the firstborn – and it becomes
the tipping point for the Israelites' exodus from Egypt.

Our passage also contains two poignant connections to Jesus.

First, the reference to a *lamb* (12:3), sacrificed to avert God's
judgement (12). The New Testament writers often described Jesus as a
lamb. The prophet who announced Jesus' arrival on the public stage,
John the Baptist, called him 'the Lamb of God' (John 1:29). Jesus'
follower Peter referred to him as a 'lamb without blemish' (1 Peter
1:19). Another follower, John, described Jesus as 'the Lamb, who was
slain' (Revelation 5:12). The Passover lamb was one of the first great
previews or trailers of God's plan of salvation.

A second connection to Jesus is the use of *blood*. Just as the blood of
the Passover lamb became the essential element that saved the
Israelites (12:7,13), so the blood of Jesus spilt as he died on the cross
was the essential element that secured salvation for all humankind.
Jesus' death was the payment demanded by a holy God in payment for
our sin. The New Testament has many references to this idea. Jesus
himself picked up this theme at the Last Supper when he offered his
followers a cup of wine as 'the new covenant in my blood'. In so doing,
he re-engineered the Passover celebration to make his salvation
available to all people (1 Corinthians 5:7).

APPLY   What does taking communion symbolise for you? Is it a
             ritual? Or a personal encounter with Jesus?

PRAY   *Just as I am, without one plea, But that Thy blood was shed
             for me, And that Thou bidd'st me come to Thee, O Lamb of
             God, I come* (from the hymn by Charlotte Elliott).

12

Date:

Trailers of a Saviour

PRAY   Father, you know there is so much on my mind today. But I just want to stop and thank you for the good things you've done in my life.

READ   Exodus 16

REFLECT

When I was growing up, our family went on some wonderful holidays together. But no matter how good the holiday had been, the journey home was always a challenge! Being cooped up for a long time in an estate car sometimes caused me and my three siblings to fuss and fight, much to my parents' frustration. That's just what happens in this passage.

God had miraculously taken the Israelites out of Egypt (12:31–42) and through the Red Sea (13:17 – 14:31). But the long journey through the desert caused them to have a family meltdown over food. Note that the word 'grumble' is mentioned seven times in the first 11 verses of this chapter. No wonder Moses finally blew his stack (16:20)!

God seems to look past the bickering of his people and again miraculously provides for them. To begin with, he gets their attention with an awesome display of his glorious presence; then he delivers the food they were yelping for. It's encouraging that God uses the Israelites' moment of weakness as an opportunity to help them grow (16:4). Thank God that he doesn't wait for us to be perfect before he'll help us!

But, embedded in this desert travelogue is another sign pointing to Jesus the Saviour. In the New Testament, when the religious leaders wanted a miracle on demand, Jesus pointed to this passage in Exodus as his answer (John 6:25–59). First, he scolded his accusers to 'stop grumbling' (John 6:43), an illusion to the Israelites in the desert they would not have missed. But then he got to the main point: just as Moses provided manna to meet the physical need of people, so he (Jesus) was the 'true bread' who satisfied the ultimate need of all people – the need for a restored and eternal relationship with God. That is Jesus' greatest miracle and he offers it to you and me.

APPLY   Where are you today in your journey with Jesus?

PRAY   Forgive me, Lord, for the times I grumble about my life. Help me focus on the good things you've given me.

13   The snakes

Date: *Trailers of a Saviour*

PRAY   'Open my eyes to see the wonderful truths in your law' (Psalm 119:18, NLT).

READ   Numbers 21:4–9

REFLECT

Alfred Hitchcock would have loved this passage! He's the famous film director who made the classic movie *The Birds*, in which people are overrun by an ominous overpopulation of black birds. Here, the Israelites are overrun by an even scarier creature: snakes! It was God's judgement for the sin of his people.

We should be careful not to 'overwork' this passage. The main offence wasn't that the Israelites were so negative; it was that they were challenging God (21:5). That's the heart of all sin.

But this episode raises a challenging question: does God cause natural disasters like plagues of snakes? The answer has two parts. First, because God created the world (Genesis 1:1) he has the power to cause or allow *anything* to happen. The Bible has many examples of this reality (Exodus 14:19–22; Matthew 8:27). But, second, we must ask: what *is* a disaster? Often God uses bad things for good purposes; in this case an infestation of snakes stopped the sinful behaviour of his people.

We may not be able to explain why some things happen in our world today, nor should we try to force a happy ending on every tragedy. Even so, we can be confident that nothing is outside God's loving purposes (Romans 8:28). His main purpose is to provide a way for people to be saved. When the Israelites looked at the bronze replica, they were saved from the effects of the poison. Note that God didn't make the snakes go away – anymore than he will always make our problems go away. His miracle was to provide a way to overcome them.

Just as the bronze snake became the vehicle for the Israelites' salvation, so Jesus' death on the cross would be the vehicle for the salvation of all people who believe in him. How amazing that God would use the complaining of a band of desert wanderers to highlight his plan of salvation for the world!

APPLY   What do you complain about most? How can you tell the difference between 'just complaining' and being angry at God?

PRAY   Lord, I don't understand some of the things that happen in my life. But I believe you love me so I ask you to open my eyes to what you are trying to teach me.

14   The new Temple

Date: *Trailers of a Saviour*

PRAY   Lord God, I worship you today. Help me to sense your presence as I read your Word and pray...

READ   1 Kings 8:1–21

REFLECT

The people of Israel have finally made it! With their captivity in Egypt a distant memory, they now have their own land and their own king. Only one thing is missing: they don't have a fitting place to worship the God of Abraham, Isaac and Jacob. But that's what makes this passage significant; it describes the 'ribbon-cutting ceremony' for the magnificent new Temple that King Solomon built in Jerusalem.

The building is impressive in its architecture (1 Kings 6) and filled with extravagant furnishings (1 Kings 7:13–51). But its true significance is what would happen there: God would be present (8:10–13). How mind-boggling that the Creator of the universe is willing to take such a step! But that reveals something important about God: he wants to meet with his people.

Over the years, the Temple was destroyed and rebuilt, and by the time of Jesus it stood at the centre of Israel's religious, political and cultural identity. It had become commercialised and out of touch with its original purpose, more like a row of tacky market stalls than a place of worship.

That's why Jesus angrily overturned the trading tables (John 2:12–17), causing the religious leaders to demand proof of his authority. In so doing, he demonstrated how this important ancient building had been pointing to him all along. 'Destroy this temple,' Jesus said, 'and I will raise it again in three days' (John 2:19). Neither his opponents nor his disciples understood. But Jesus meant that, as a result of his death and resurrection, *he* would replace Solomon's Temple as the way to God. After that, meeting God would no longer be for the high priest behind a thick curtain (Matthew 27:51). It would be available to every believer who trusts in Jesus.

APPLY   How could your church become more like a place to meet God and less like a shopping centre? When do your feel God's presence the most?

PRAY   Dear God, help me focus my mind and heart on how powerful and loving you are.

15

Running on empty

Date:

PRAY   Dear God, I believe that everything happens for a reason. And I'm so grateful that you know what it is.

READ   Jonah 1 – 4

REFLECT

Everyone knows the basic story of Jonah, but it's still a fun read. Jonah was a man called by God to preach a message of judgement to the wicked people in Nineveh. Maybe Jonah was prejudiced against people outside his own community, or maybe he wanted to be popular, or maybe he was just afraid of violent repercussions. Whatever his reason, Jonah foolishly tried to run from God. But that's no more foolish than the way we behave, when we think that we can engage in 'secret sin'. God always knows.

God also has a way of getting our secrets out into the open. One way is through our consciences (1:10). The fact that we have a conscience at all is indirect proof that God exists. Where did our sense of right and wrong come from in the first place? Other evidence of God's existence is his intervention in our circumstances; in Jonah's case, he was swallowed by a 'great fish' (1:17). That particular event may never happen to you, but God *will* allow things in your life for a reason. That's why it's always good to ask, 'Lord, what are you trying to say to me through this?'

When the sceptical religious leaders of his day asked for miraculous proof of his authenticity, Jesus referred to this Old Testament book (Matthew 12:38–45). In essence he was saying that the story of Jonah provided all the proof they needed. How? Just as Jonah was entombed in the great fish for three days, so Jesus would be in the tomb three days after his death by crucifixion. And Jesus would rise again. Just as the great fish gave up Jonah, so the grave would give up Jesus. The bottom line is: Jesus didn't come to impress people with magic tricks. He came to set them free from sin through his death and resurrection.

APPLY   Is there any area of your life in which you are 'running from God' right now? Why, and what do you think you should do about it?

PRAY   Lord, you know all about it when I go through tough times and I don't have all the answers. Help me to know what you are trying to say to me.

DISCUSSION QUESTIONS: TRAILERS OF A SAVIOUR

After you've completed the five readings in this section, get together with another person or group to talk about the things you've learned. Begin by sharing the insights you gained from your own reflection on the passages. Then use the following questions to help you continue the conversation.

1   Which of the five Old Testament stories that we considered in this section taught you the most about Jesus Christ? Why?

2   How did this section affect your view of the Old Testament? Of the Bible?

3   Can you think of any popular books, television programmes or films that present Bible stories? Do you think they give a balanced portrayal of Jesus?

4   For you, what are the most significant Christian symbols? (The cross? Bread and wine?) Why?

5   In today's society, which do you think are most effective in communicating the truth about Jesus: symbols, examples, teaching, preaching or... ?

PSALMS ABOUT A SAVIOUR

The Book of Psalms is one of the most loved and most read sections of the entire Bible. It contains the prayers, poems, praises and laments of some passionate servants of God from the past: people like David, Solomon, Moses, Asaph (the 'worship leader' during David's lifetime) and several others.

Another feature that makes the Psalms so rich in meaning is that they continue the developing storyline about Jesus Christ that we've already seen in earlier parts of the Bible. These Psalms are often called 'Messianic Psalms' because they may be seen as 'trailers' of the coming Saviour or Messiah. The Psalms that many have seen as specifically pointing to the Messiah are Psalms 2, 8, 16, 22, 24, 40, 41, 45, 69, 72, 89, 102, 110 and 118. If you have the time, you may want to read all of these psalms in one sitting to get the full impact.

To give us a good sense of what these special Psalms are all about, we will read five of the most popular ones; in so doing we'll gain several insights that instruct us today.

First, we'll discover that Jesus often quoted from the Psalms, which reminds us that when we read the Old Testament, we're reading the same Bible Jesus read. And what's obvious is that Jesus studied and memorised the Scriptures; that's a good example for us.

Second, we'll discover that these Psalms give us an amazingly graphic picture of what would happen to Jesus – a dynamic we'll experience again in the parts of the Bible we call the prophetic books. One of the most famous Messianic Psalms is Psalm 22, the one Jesus quoted on the cross: 'My God, my God, why have you forsaken me?' But, even more striking is the detailed description of a crucifixion that it contains, which reminds us that the cross was no accident. God knew all along how he planned to offer salvation to the world, and to you.

So get ready to dig into the Psalms about a Saviour!

16   The case for Christ

Date: *Psalms about a Saviour*

PRAY   Heavenly Father, I'd like to be as close to you as a child feels towards a loving parent.

READ   Psalm 2

REFLECT

From 1945 to 1991, the Soviet Union was one of two superpowers in the world. Yet, in spite of a strong central government and a feared military capability, the USSR had a fatal flaw: rejection of God. Atheism was its official policy and Christianity was brutally suppressed. In the end, it wasn't a nuclear confrontation that toppled the mighty Communist regime. Rather, it was undone by the faithful witness and courageous resistance of the Church.

That would come as no surprise to the writer of this psalm, whose intent was to advise the kings of Israel on the key to successful leadership. Foolish kings 'conspire' and 'plot' to banish God from his earth (2:1–3). Laughable as that may seem, especially to God (2:4), this still happens today. Increasingly, western democracies are forgetting that their ultimate authority is God, not the majority. Regardless of the political system, any nation that forgets God is heading for trouble. Wise leaders, on the other hand, serve the Lord (2:11) and reap the benefits of doing so for themselves and their people (2:8,9).

But there's more to this psalm than meets the eye. Viewed from the perspective of the New Testament we see several phrases that point to Jesus. The psalm's description of a father's approval of his son (7) echoes what God would later say at Jesus' public baptism or dipping by John the Baptist in the River Jordan (Matthew 3:17). And the name given to Jesus – Messiah – means 'Anointed One', the very phrase used here (2:2). When the early Christians Peter and John were being persecuted for speaking about Jesus after his resurrection and ascension, they quoted this psalm (Acts 4:25,26). Put it all together and we realise that, centuries before Jesus appeared, the Holy Spirit was already developing a case for Christ.

APPLY   In what ways do countries reject God today? What are some effective and ineffective ways leaders attempt to bring God into politics? Should God be part of the political process?

PRAY   Lord Jesus, regardless of what others do, I desire to follow you. Help me to influence others in your direction today.

17

At the cross

Date:

Psalms about a Saviour

PRAY   Dear God, I'm hungry for a deeper understanding of your love for me today.

READ   Psalm 22

REFLECT

It's not difficult to see how this psalm relates to Jesus; it's a vivid description of what Jesus experienced at his crucifixion. In fact, Jesus quoted this very psalm while he hung on the cross: 'My God, my God, why have you forsaken me?' (22:1; Mark 15:34). No doubt Jesus memorised these words as he grew up. 'Hiding God's word in our hearts', as this act of memorising is poetically described in Psalm 119:11, may seem like a specialist spiritual discipline, but it can become a reservoir of spiritual strength in times of trial for any believer.

To fully appreciate this psalm, we need to consider what it meant in its original context. Written by David, it describes the inner feelings of a man in trouble – big trouble. Have you ever faced a problem so great, so devastating, that it affected your attitude, your activities, your health and everything in your world? That's how David is feeling here.

One of David's great strengths was his ability to communicate his feelings. Another was his reflex for turning to God when the chips were down. He did this by making himself remember what God had done in the past (22:4), which gave him hope and enabled him to trust. He also took time out for praising (22:25) and worshipping God (22:29) in the middle of the crisis. That's how David weathered the storms in his life and what made him 'a man after God's own heart' (Acts 13:22).

How could it be that, nearly a thousand years before Jesus lived, David could predict the specific details of the way Jesus would die (22:16; John 19:24–29), or what would happen at the foot of the cross (22:18; John 19:24,25) or even what Jesus' enemies would say (22:8; Matthew 27:41–43)? The only answer can be that God inspired David to write what he did (2 Timothy 3:16,17; Acts 1:16). The Bible, uniquely, is God's book and Jesus is the main character from start to finish.

APPLY   How do you react when the bottom drops out of your world? How has God helped you in past times of trouble?

PRAY   Lord Jesus, it's hard for me to imagine what you went through on the cross. All I can say is thank you, thank you, thank you.

18   Deep waters

Date: *Psalms about a Saviour*

PRAY   Father, please give me a deeper sense of your presence and your priorities as I read your Word today.

READ   Psalm 69

REFLECT

The Psalms have always been most meaningful to me when I've been in trouble. I remember once being part of a financial collapse in a ministry; it was so overwhelming I thought I'd never get out. On the outside, I was going through the motions of normal life. But, inside, all I could think about was the looming crisis. In my desperation, I read the Psalms over and over; it was enormously helpful to read the heart cries of people who had nowhere else to turn but to God.

That's what's happening here. David is in 'deep waters' (69:2,14) and is calling out for God's help. It's not clear what particular problem David faced, but he had got himself into a jam. Note how David responds to his overwhelming problem:

He honestly describes the situation to God (69:1–4).

He examines his own heart instead of pointing fingers at others (69:5,6).

He makes his request known to God (69:13–18), and takes time to praise God (69:30–36).

This psalm was especially meaningful to Jesus; he quoted it when explaining why the world hated him and his followers (John 15:25), and no doubt saw his own suffering on the cross echoed in the statement, 'they persecute those you wound' (69:26). And it turns out that the references to gall and vinegar (69:21) are prophetic of the details of Jesus' death (Matthew 27:34,45). The disciples too were familiar with this psalm, seeing it as an explanation for Jesus' clearing of the Temple (John 2:17).

Take a minute to read these verses one more time and marvel at how they've spoken so poignantly to struggling people down through the ages – whether they be David, Jesus, the disciples, me or you.

APPLY   Sometimes God uses a crisis to expose the sins we've been unable or unwilling to confess to him. Are you facing something like that right now? Ask God for his help.

PRAY   Lord, I'm so thankful that I don't have to be perfect for you to help me or to love me. Forgive me for not turning to you first when I get in a jam.

19

Who's talking?

Date:

Psalms about a Saviour

PRAY   'I rejoice in following your statutes as one rejoices in great riches' (Psalm 119:14).

READ   Psalm 110

REFLECT

I've always found this a confusing psalm. Who's doing the talking? It seems as if there are two 'Lords' (110:1). And what's the main point? It seems a jumble of biblical allusions. Yet the New Testament refers to this Psalm more than any other. What's so important about these seven verses?

It begins to make sense when you see that the psalm is built around two direct statements from God in verses 1 and 4, each followed by David's commentary on what God has said. Next, it helps to consider what this psalm meant to its original hearers. Over the years, it would have been recited to honour the royal descendants of King David at various special occasions. From that perspective, the first section (110:1–3) is an affirmation of the king's power. God (the LORD) is inviting the king (my Lord) to sit next to him. The second section (110:4–7) affirms the king's unique spiritual leadership. Melchizedek was both King of Jerusalem and 'the priest of God Most High' who blessed Abraham (Genesis 14:18–20).

But the most significant thing about this psalm is the way it points to the coming Messiah. Jesus quoted these verses to challenge the religious leaders who doubted he was the Son of God (Matthew 22:41–45). They thought the Messiah would be merely a human descendant of David. But Jesus demonstrated, by referring to this psalm, that the Messiah would also be the divine Son of God. He then applied all of that symbolism to himself. In other words, Jesus was saying *he* was the Messiah, the divine/ human Saviour of the world.

Once we sort through the complexity of this short psalm we are left with a simple fact: Jesus is the Son of God – the essential message of the entire Bible.

APPLY   How certain are you that Jesus was who he said he was: the Son of God and Saviour of the world?

PRAY   Lord Jesus, there are many things about you I don't fully understand. But I believe that you love me and I thank you for that.

20   Try to remember

Date: *Psalms about a Saviour*

PRAY   Lord, I've got a million things swirling in my mind right now. But what I want most is to know and experience more of you.

READ   Psalm 118

REFLECT

This passage contains one of 'the greatest hits' from the Psalms: 'This is the day the LORD has made; let us rejoice and be glad in it' has become the opening sentence for countless worship services and songs around the world.

Originally the words commemorated an unspecified victory in Jewish history. Apparently God's people had been in a 'backs against the wall' situation, from which God had miraculously delivered them (118:5–14). That produced this unrestrained expression of joy and praise to God (118:14–28).

When are you the most enthusiastic about praising God? People who have most recently experienced God's help are often the most energetic about praising him. That's why it's important to remember what God has done for us. It keeps our faith joyful and alive.

In the middle of this celebration of God's past deliverance, however, are two references to an even greater deliverance he planned for the future:

'The stone the builders rejected has become the capstone…' Jesus quoted this verse at the end of his parable about the tenants who killed the vineyard owner's son (Matthew 21:33–46). His point? That he, Jesus, was the stone the religious leaders had rejected, but whom God would make into the cornerstone (foundation) of his Church.

'Blessed is he who comes in the name of the LORD' was one of the phrases shouted by the crowds during Jesus' triumphal entry into Jerusalem a week before his death on the cross (Matthew 21:1–11).

The greater deliverance God had in mind was his plan to save the world from sin and to offer people relationship with him. That was accomplished on the cross.

APPLY   Have you ever been in a 'back against the wall' situation? Did you remember to pray for God's help? What happened?

PRAY   Take a few minutes to thank God joyfully for any ways he's helped you out of sticky situations in your life.

DISCUSSION QUESTIONS: PSALMS ABOUT A SAVIOUR

After you've completed the five readings in this section, get together with another person or group to talk about the things you've learned. Begin by sharing the insights you gained from your own reflection on the passages. Then use the following questions to help you continue the conversation.

1   Which of the five psalms in this section communicated the most to you about Jesus Christ? Why?

2   How would you respond to someone who said, 'Any comparison to Jesus in the Psalms is purely coincidence'?

3   Why do you think Jesus read and memorised Scripture? Can you think of other times when his biblical knowledge helped him or was significant in any way?

4   Have you ever tried to memorise a verse or passage of Scripture? How did it go? Can you recite a favourite verse now?

5   What motivates you most to read the Bible? When has the Bible meant the most to you in your life? Why?

6   What do you find are the biggest obstacles to reading the Bible regularly? How could you overcome them?

7   Many people find that the Bible becomes more meaningful when they are in a crisis. Why do you suppose that is so? Has it ever been your experience?

PROPHECIES ABOUT A SAVIOUR

When you think about 'prophecy', what comes to mind? Perhaps you think of an exciting film where the protagonist unwittingly stumbles into a perplexing set of events that trace back to some weird and ancient prophecy. Or maybe you think of a fairground psychic whose sign claims she can tell you about your future in love, business and life – for a mere £5. Or maybe you think of a religious extremist who predicts the end of the world in a new book and speaking tour.

Whatever you think about prophecy, it's important to understand that the Bible takes it very seriously and contains lots of it. In fact, there are 17 prophetic books in the Old Testament: five longer ones called the 'major' prophets and 12 shorter ones or 'minor' prophets.

So what exactly is biblical prophecy? At its heart it's about proclaiming God's truth in a particular situation or *'forth-telling'*. Over the years, God's people (the Israelites) developed some very sinful habits, including idol worship, corruption and oppression of the poor. The prophets forcefully articulated what God's standards were and how he wanted his people to live.

Another aspect of biblical prophecy involves predicting God's plan for the future or *'fore-telling'*. In the Old Testament one of the most common themes of the prophetic books is that of a coming day of judgement: 'the day of the Lord'. Many of the prophets warned God's people that their idolatry and sin would eventually bring punishment. These prophecies all came true when Babylon destroyed Jerusalem and took God's people into exile in 586 BC.

Of course, an important feature of biblical prophecy is that whether it involved forth-telling or fore-telling, it was not just the words and thoughts of a man. As Peter said, 'For prophecy never had its origin in the will of man, but men spoke from God as they were carried along by the Holy Spirit.' A prophet was someone who spoke for God.

But there's something else about Old Testament prophecy that will be the focus of our next five readings. It frequently predicted the coming of a Messiah who would bring God's salvation to earth. We'll start by examining the first hint we get of this theme in the book of Genesis. We'll then read a few of the hundreds of specific predictions about this 'Anointed One' scattered throughout the prophetic books. By the time we complete this section perhaps for you there will be no mystery – you may be convinced that Jesus Christ perfectly fulfilled every prophecy about the coming Messiah!

21

Chosen people

Date:

Prophecies about a Saviour

PRAY   Father, make my mind sharp and my heart open as I think about your Word today.

READ   Genesis 12:1–9

REFLECT

The Bible got off to a great start: God created a perfect world and Adam and Eve had a perfect life. But sin changed all that. Humanity quickly found itself separated from God and trapped in a wicked world spiralling out of control (6:5). Society's not very different today! But this passage marks a new beginning in God's dealings with people.

We don't get much background on Abraham. When he was 75 years old he stepped out in obedience to God to go to an unknown land (12:1). Regardless of your age, could you let go of everything to follow God's call? His willingness to abandon himself to God made Abraham one of the greatest examples of faith in the entire Bible (15:6).

Abraham's call was no random act of unkindness. God was putting in motion an incredible plan to reverse the effects of sin and to give people a way to have close fellowship with him once again. Here, God only gives a short summary of what he had in mind (12:2,3). It would take thousands of years for his plan of salvation to unfold fully.

The plan had two major components.

God would create 'a great nation' (12:2) from Abraham's family, who would eventually become the Israelites. God uniquely revealed himself to these people over centuries, through a variety of incredible experiences and miracles, and eventually through the Ten Commandments and the Law. Through it all, the people began to understand who God was and how he wanted them to live.

God would bless 'all the peoples on earth' (12:3) through these 'chosen people'. The great blessing was to be Jesus Christ, the Saviour of the world.

But at this point, Abraham had no idea what God had in mind. All he knew was that God said 'Go' and so he did. It's amazing what God can do through one person who is willing to trust and obey him.

APPLY   Does anything hold you back from wholeheartedly following Jesus?

PRAY   Lord, I don't want to follow you out of a sense of guilt or duty. But I do want to grow a greater trust in you and your purposes for me.

22   The Good Shepherd

Date: *Prophecies about a Saviour*

PRAY   Lord, there are so many problems in the world and even in my life. But, no matter what, I can always praise you for how good and great and loving you are.

READ   Jeremiah 23:1–9

REFLECT

After God announced his plan to bless all nations of the world through his chosen people (Genesis 12:2,3), it would be nice to think they lived 'happily ever after'. But, as the Bible shows us, it didn't work out that way. The Israelites couldn't resist the temptation to do things *their* way instead of God's (that's the short definition of sin); and it got them into all kinds of trouble.

Jeremiah was one of the prophets God sent to denounce Israel's sin and turn them back to God. It wasn't a job he really wanted (Jeremiah 1:4–19) and it caused him a lot of grief (Jeremiah 20). But Jeremiah faithfully expressed God's perspective to the people around him. As then, our world desperately needs men and women who will 'speak the truth in love' (Ephesians 4:15) in spite of the consequences.

One group who especially felt the heat of Jeremiah's prophecy were the religious leaders – the 'shepherds' (23:1,2). We know from other parts of this book that they were following a path of idolatry, injustice and immorality instead of truly caring for the people. In response, God says he's going to defrock the religious leaders and take the reins himself ('I myself… ', 23:3). That should be a wake-up call to the leaders of God's people in any age.

It also opens the door for another prophecy or foretelling about God's plan. Jeremiah tells us that the Saviour would not only be a descendant of David but also something more – a righteous (just, holy) Branch (23:5) and the Lord our Righteousness (23:6). In other words, God was planning to step into the picture to re-establish the right relationship between us and him that sin had destroyed. He would do this by sending his own son, Jesus Christ. The tragic impact of these 'bad' shepherds has a good purpose in God's plan – they highlight the need for the Good Shepherd (John 10:11–18).

APPLY   Is there a difficult situation in your life where you need to 'speak the truth in love'? How could you do this?

PRAY   Jesus, help me to see the difference between *my* way and *your* way of doing things in some of the difficult areas of my life.

23   'O Little Town of Bethlehem'

Date: *Prophecies about a Saviour*

PRAY   'Praise the LORD, O my soul; all my inmost being, praise his holy name' (Psalm 103:1).

READ   Micah 5:1–5

REFLECT

Micah was no TV preacher. His messages weren't slick, packaged or positive. They were rough, passionate and hard-hitting (see, for example, 3:1–4). And he would have been a terrible fundraiser because his main theme was to denounce sin, especially that of the wealthy and powerful. 'Come on, man. You'll never build a donor base like that!' we might say. But Micah wasn't trying to be popular; he was trying to be faithful to the message he had been given (1:1). God was going to punish Israel for her sins. Micah's prophecy was fulfilled when Babylon destroyed Jerusalem and took the people into captivity.

Buried in the middle of his challenging prophetic book, however, we find our passage – one of the most significant in the Old Testament. In it, Micah looks beyond his current situation to a time far, far in the future when God would send a Saviour whose rule would extend to 'the ends of the earth' (5:4). Even in these few verses we learn several important details about this coming Saviour, all of which were fulfilled by Jesus Christ.

His origins The Saviour would come from the little town of Bethlehem (5:2). At the time of Jesus' birth, this was the commonly held understanding (Matthew 2:3–6). It was such an unlikely place, and yet God orchestrated an incredible chain of events – a census of the Roman empire, a journey by a pregnant woman and her fiancé, and a birth in a stable – to make it happen (Luke 2:1–7).

His character Micah picks up on the shepherd imagery, as have other prophets. But he adds that the Saviour's strength and majesty won't be based on human ability but rather on 'the name of the LORD his God' (5:4). And the Saviour won't just achieve a time of peace, but 'he will be their peace' (5:5). Micah was prophesying about none other than Jesus Christ who made peace (that is, restored our relationship) with God by his death on the cross.

APPLY   Do you feel that you're at peace with God?

PRAY   Thank you, Jesus, that because of your death I can know forgiveness, freedom from guilt, and closeness to God.

24   The humble King

Date: *Prophecies about a Saviour*

PRAY   Father, help me quiet my mind and heart so I can hear what you want to say to me…

READ   Zechariah 9:9–17

REFLECT

Many Old Testament prophets warned of a coming day of judgement, which finally arrived with the fall of Jerusalem and Israel's exile into Babylon in 586 BC. Zechariah lived after these terrible events, at a time when Israel had been allowed to return to their land. In the first part of his prophesy (chapters 1–8) Zechariah encourages the people to continue rebuilding the Temple and to avoid falling into the sin patterns of the past. In the second part (chapters 9–14) he looks forward to the coming of a very special King. The question is, what kind of king would he be?

After living in captivity for over 70 years, it was natural for the Israelites to want a strong king, someone who would fight fire with fire. But revenge and violence only make things worse, as the history of the Middle East and our own relationships clearly prove. The king Zechariah described was very different from anyone Israel had seen or experienced:

He would be *humble* (9:9), not proud or arrogant. He would establish genuine *peace* throughout the world (9:10), not just the protection of Israel. He would bring in a new kind of *freedom*, one based on 'the blood of my covenant with you' (9:11).

It's not hard to see how these prophecies were fulfilled, starting five centuries later: Jesus was *humble* – he entered Jerusalem riding on a donkey (Matthew 21:1–11); he was the epitome of a servant leader (John 13:1–17). Jesus brought *freedom* – by dying on the cross, Jesus freed people from the prison of sin and enabled them to be reconciled to God (Ephesians 1:7). Jesus will bring *peace* – someday in the future, he will come again to establish an everlasting peace for those who believe in him (1 Thessalonians 4:16,17).

So, Jesus Christ *was and is* the Saviour King God promised through Zechariah so many years ago.

APPLY   How could you demonstrate in your own life the kind of humility Jesus showed?

PRAY   Spend some time praying for the people who you feel have wronged you most recently…

25

Future clues

Date:

Prophecies about a Saviour

PRAY   Lord God, please help me hear your voice as I read and reflect on this passage today.

READ   Zechariah 12,13

REFLECT

How do Bible books like Zechariah, or any of the Old Testament prophets, connect with life today? After all, they describe ancient times that are completely unfamiliar to us now. Plus they all have such weird names!

The answer is: They show us what God is like. By reading how he reacted to particular situations in the past, we learn how he wants us to live today. In addition, the prophetic books often contain clues or references to more significant events in the future.

That's what we find in our passage today. It describes a time when Jerusalem would be surrounded and outnumbered by her enemies (12:2,3) – sadly, a situation that has occurred often throughout history. But Israel will prevail, Zechariah says – not because of her own power, but rather 'because the LORD Almighty is their God' (12:5). That's true for us today; the ultimate source of our safety and success is not our own strength and abilities. Rather it's God's work on our behalf, which is why praise is so appropriate and pride so outrageous.

Our passage also contains several of the future clues that make the prophetic books so relevant. One is Zechariah's reference to 'the one they have pierced' (12:10). In his Gospel account, John linked this verse to Jesus' death on the cross (John 19:36,37). It was the event that provided the cleansing from sin which Zechariah anticipated (13:1). Another future clue is found in the poem about the shepherd and the sheep (13:7–9). Jesus quoted this very passage to predict how Peter and the other disciples would desert him at his arrest (Matthew 26:31–35).

One other thing that makes the ancient prophetic books come alive today is that they often quote God directly, such as: 'This is the word of the LORD... ' (12:1). God spoke to the prophets and they wrote it down (that's what an 'oracle' is, 12:1). And when God speaks, we'd better listen!

APPLY   Today, could you look out more for the ways God is working in your life? And praise him for it?

PRAY   Thank you that you are a God who has spoken in the past and who continues to speak today.

DISCUSSION QUESTIONS: PROPHECIES ABOUT A SAVIOUR

After you've completed the five readings in this section, get together with another person or group to talk about the things you've learned. Begin by sharing the insights you gained from your own reflection on the passages. Then use the following questions to help you continue the conversation.

1   How do you see the idea of prophecy ('forth-telling' or 'fore-telling') portrayed in popular culture today?

2   What is your view of prophecy? How would you describe it in your own words?

3   Do you think people today make too much or too little of biblical prophecy? Why and how does it make a difference?

4   Which of the prophecies in this section is the most significant for you in terms of the argument that Jesus was the Messiah? Why?

5   Do you think there are any genuine prophets in the world today – people who are 'forth-tellers' or 'fore-tellers' on behalf of God? Discuss your experiences and insights.

MORE PROPHECIES ABOUT A SAVIOUR

When it comes to the Old Testament prophets, Isaiah is up there with the celebrities. For one thing, he was active for somewhere between 40 and 60 years, his ministry outlasting four kings. For another, his book is the longest of all the prophets – 66 big chapters in all – and is the prophetic book most quoted in the New Testament. But the hugely significant thing about Isaiah is that his prophecy gives us the most information about the coming Deliverer, which is why we'll spend the next five readings pursuing what the Lord said through him.

The clearest descriptions of this Deliverer are found in four so-called 'Servant Songs' in the book of Isaiah (they are 42:1–9; 49:1–6; 50:4–9; 52:13 – 53:12). They all describe various aspects of 'the Servant of the LORD'. Who exactly is this servant? Scholars love to debate questions like that, but for our purposes we can boil it down to this: the phrase refers both to the nation of Israel *and* the coming Messiah.

Looking ahead to the New Testament, you'll see that Jesus took the 'Servant of the LORD' mantle on himself at the beginning of his ministry by quoting from one of the Servant Songs. 'The scroll of the prophet Isaiah was handed to him. Unrolling it, he found the place where it is written:

> The Spirit of the Lord is on me,
>   because he has anointed me
>   to preach good news to the poor.
> He has sent me to proclaim freedom for the prisoners
>   and recovery of sight for the blind,
>   to release the oppressed,
>   to proclaim the year of the Lord's favour.

The eyes of everyone in the synagogue were fastened on him as he said, 'Today this scripture is fulfilled in your hearing' (Luke 4:17–21). Jesus was keenly aware that Isaiah had prophesied about him; it was a fact that guided his ministry on earth.

But perhaps the most famous passage in the book of Isaiah is the description of the 'suffering servant' (52:13 – 53:12). God inspired Isaiah to describe the crucifixion of Jesus in graphic detail long before it happened. It's hard to imagine that the God of the universe would send his own Son to die for the sins of humankind, but that's exactly what he did – and just what Isaiah prophesied about *eight hundred years before* it happened.

26 God with us

Date: *More prophecies about a Saviour*

PRAY   Father, my heart's desire is to experience your presence
              in a fresh way today.

READ   Isaiah 7

REFLECT

This passage contains one of the most well-known and debated
prophecies about the coming Messiah in the entire Old Testament.
Isaiah says that a virgin will give birth to a son called Emmanuel,
which literally means 'God with us' (7:14). The New Testament makes
clear this prophecy was fulfilled in the birth of Jesus Christ (Matthew
1:18–25). But to understand these verses fully, we need to consider
what they meant to the original hearers.

Since 925 BC, God's chosen people had been split into two rival
kingdoms: Judah in the south and Israel in the north. At the beginning
of this chapter we learn that Pekah, king of Israel, and Rezin, king of
Aram (Syria), are attacking King Ahaz in Jerusalem, the capital of the
Southern Kingdom. God's message is reassuring: 'Stay calm. I will
deal with Pekah and Rezin.'

When we find ourselves facing battles today – at work, in the
community or even in the church – we need to remember that,
ultimately, 'success' is dependent on God, not on our cleverness or
political skill (7:9).

For many years I worked in an outreach ministry called Prison
Fellowship with the founder, former White House aide Chuck Colson,
who had been himself imprisoned in the Nixon years and then
converted to Christ. On Chuck's desk was a plaque that read
Faithfulness, not success.

Trusting God when the pressure is on can be tough. God promised
the birth of a son named Emmanuel. For the original hearers, this
probably meant that when God delivered Judah from their attackers,
young mothers would name their sons in memory of God's
deliverance, just as Isaiah had named his son after a future deliverance
of God. But the sign also predicted God's greatest deliverance –
sending his own Son Jesus Christ to deliver all people from sin. The
great miracle is that because of Jesus' entry into human history, God is
with us for ever.

APPLY   Are you facing situations of pressure at work, in the
              community or in your church? What would a successful
              response look like? And a faithful response?

PRAY   Ask Jesus to help you remain faithful to him, whatever
              you face today.

27   Hope for the future

Date: *More prophecies about a Saviour*

PRAY   Lord, renew my sense of true joy as I spend time with you today.

READ   Isaiah 9:1–7

REFLECT

Here, Isaiah gives God's people a message of hope. They sure needed it! As we discovered in Isaiah 7, Jerusalem was being attacked by two armies. God delivered his people from that threat only to allow an even bigger one: the powerful nation of Assyria would soon attack as punishment for their sin (7:17; 8:6–8).

It's natural to want God to solve the problems we find ourselves in. He can and often does. But what he really cares about is that we have a right relationship with him. Sometimes that means he allows us to go through trials to strengthen our faith. Sometimes it means he allows painful experiences to expose our hidden sins. But all the time he is at work for our good.

That's why the word 'nevertheless' is such a hopeful start to chapter 9. In spite of Judah's sin and troubles, God was planning something good. Not only would he take away their gloom and distress but also he would give them a future that would be wonderful in at least three ways:

Light God would turn their darkness into light (9:2). In other words, he was promising eventual deliverance from the Assyrian invasion.

Joy This deliverance would lead to unrestrained joy (9:3). When God intervenes to solve our problems, it's hard not to praise him with abandon.

The coming of the Messiah Finally, a child would be born who would become a unique leader (9:6,7) – the promised Messiah. This prophecy was fulfilled in Jesus Christ, who delivered us from the darkness of sin and established an everlasting kingdom for those who put their trust in him.

Having hope does not mean being without problems, as God's people have discovered throughout the ages. Rather, it is knowing that God is there and in control – no matter what happens.

APPLY   Are there ways in which the past and present circumstances of your life have drawn you to Jesus?

PRAY   Jesus, I'm so thankful for your involvement in my life...

28   Chosen servant

Date: *More prophecies about a Saviour*

PRAY   Spend some time confessing your sins to God and then thanking him for his forgiveness.

READ   Isaiah 42:1–9

REFLECT

This passage is the first of the four Servant Songs which we find throughout the book of Isaiah (see page 48). At the time Isaiah uttered this prophecy, no doubt he was thinking of the nation of Israel. But God was also communicating some important truths about the coming Messiah:

He is chosen by God. Israel had been chosen by God long ago when God promised to make Abram's family into a great nation (Genesis 12:2). Isaiah prophesied that one day a Saviour would come who would be uniquely chosen by God.

He is God's instrument of salvation. From the very birth of the chosen people, God's intent was to bring blessing to all people through them (Genesis 12:3). Isaiah builds on his theme, saying that the servant would be filled with the Spirit of God and establish justice for all, including the weak and downtrodden – the 'bruised reeds' and 'smouldering wicks' (42:3).

At his baptism, Jesus was filled with the Holy Spirit (Matthew 3:16); by his death and resurrection he provided the way of salvation for all people. Jesus himself said that he was the fulfilment of this passage (Matthew 12:15–21). When the Pharisees were out to kill him, Jesus used this passage to explain to his disciples who he was – God's promised Messiah.

By the time we get to the New Testament we'll see confirmation that the Saviour promised in the Old Testament was none other than Jesus Christ.

APPLY   Who are the weak and downtrodden in your community, the 'bruised reeds' and 'smouldering wicks'? How could you join with Jesus to be an instrument of justice for them?

PRAY   Jesus, help me to love justice just as you do.

29   **Man of sorrows**

Date: *More prophecies about a Saviour*

PRAY   Father, open my heart to what you want to say to me in the next few minutes.

READ   Isaiah 52:13 – 53:12

REFLECT

This passage describes the 'suffering servant' and in the process gives us a detailed picture of what Jesus would experience on the cross. What's amazing is that Isaiah wrote these verses about eight hundred years before Jesus lived! That highlights the unique nature of the Bible; it was inspired by God (2 Timothy 3:16).

The odd thing is that the people closest to Jesus – his disciples – missed the point. They wanted a conquering hero, not a suffering servant. It's easy to make the same mistake today. We assume God will work through the power structures of our day, so we spend a lot of time and energy trying to influence them. But the truth is, God often prefers to use the weak and the lowly to accomplish his purposes in the world (Luke 1:46–55).

So what details about this unique servant did the Holy Spirit reveal to Isaiah?

The servant would have to suffer (53:3,7,10). It was the 'LORD's will to crush him and cause him to suffer' (53:10).

The servant's suffering would pay for the sins of others (53:5,6,12). That's the key to this passage and it's exactly what Jesus did on the cross.

The suffering servant would eventually be restored and glorified (53:11,12), which is what happened when Jesus was brought back to life after being crucified and put in the tomb.

Isaiah couldn't have understood the full implications of what he prophesied and it took a while for the first Christians to figure it out (1 Peter 2:21–25). But now we have the great advantage of seeing the full picture of God's plan of salvation. The challenge for us is, how do we respond?

APPLY   Are you proud of your self-sufficiency – or weak enough for God to use?

PRAY   Spend some time prayerfully responding to what Jesus did on the cross. You might want to admit your questions and doubts or maybe for the first time say, 'Yes, I believe... ' or from the depths of your heart thank Jesus for saving you.

30

Mission statement

More prophecies about a Saviour

PRAY   Do I think too much about the glass being half-empty? Lord, open my eyes to the good things you are doing in my life.

READ   Isaiah 61

REFLECT

Time for some good news! After all the gloom, doom and suffering described by the prophets so far, it's nice to read about freedom, comfort and a time of 'the LORD's favour'. Ah… now that feels better.

But this is much more than a 'feel-good' passage. God never abandons his people. As we've discovered, the Israelites had been attacked and taken captive by powerful nations around them. Their key city and Temple had been destroyed. All of it happened because they had sinned against God. But here, Isaiah describes a time when everything would be put right and the Israelites' despair would be turned to praise (61:3).

This underscores two aspects of God's character:

He is a God of hope. Regardless of what we've done, regardless of what mess we make of our life, with God we can have a fresh start and a new future. That doesn't mean all our trials magically go away; some problems take years to be resolved, some never completely disappear. But, even so, God is always at work for our ultimate good (Jeremiah 29:11–13), just as he was for the Israelites.

He passionately loves justice and hates sin (61:8). The surest way to experience God's blessing is to be passionate about his priorities.

This passage had special significance for Jesus; as we have seen, he used it as the mission statement for his life on earth (Luke 4:18,19).

Jesus came to offer God's forgiveness and hope to those held captive to sin and to bring God's justice to the poor and oppressed. That's the good news!

APPLY   How would you describe the mission statement for your life? If you can, take a few minutes to write it down.

PRAY   Lord Jesus, I want my life to count for you. Please help me see clearly whatever mission you've called me to and help me accomplish it.

DISCUSSION QUESTIONS: MORE PROPHECIES ABOUT A SAVIOUR

After you've completed the five readings in this section, get together with another person or group to talk about the things you've learned. Begin by sharing the insights you gained from your own reflection on the passages. Then use the following questions to help you continue the conversation.

1   Which of the prophecies in this section is the most significant persuasion for you that Jesus was the Messiah?

2   The people of Israel felt the pressure of hostile armies on all sides; Jesus felt the incredible pressure of being misunderstood, opposed and eventually betrayed and crucified. What pressures do you face for your beliefs and how do you cope?

3   Have you ever felt that God has abandoned you? When? And when do you most feel that God is with you?

4   Is there anything that tempts you to give up hope about the future? In contrast, what gives you most hope for the future?

5   Jesus said he came to bring good news to the poor, the prisoners, blind and oppressed. How could you be more like Jesus in this regard?

6   Jesus seemed to claim the passage in Isaiah 61 as his personal mission statement. What's yours? (You may want to share your notes from reading 30.)

THE BIRTH OF JESUS

Since 1965 when it first appeared as a television special, *A Charlie Brown Christmas* has possibly done more to communicate the essence of the gospel than any 30-minute sermon ever has! In the programme, Charlie Brown – the cartoon character from the Peanuts comic strip – searches for the true meaning of Christmas, only to be disappointed and disillusioned. Finally, Charlie's thumb-sucking friend Linus walks onto an empty stage and recites from the Gospel of Luke, 'For unto you is born this day in the city of David a Saviour, which is Christ the Lord' (Luke 2:11, KJV). Linus finishes by simply saying, 'And that's what Christmas is all about, Charlie Brown.'

In spite of the growing commercialisation and secularisation of 'the holiday season', most people today are still hungry to know what Christmas is all about. And that's exactly what our next five readings on the birth of Jesus will help us understand. We'll cover the familiar story of Joseph and Mary trekking to Bethlehem, a birth in an unlikely setting, and the shepherds, angels and heavenly hosts all welcoming this special child.

One thing you'll notice is that the birth of Jesus was definitely not a random act; we see God clearly at work orchestrating this wonderful event. Several times God sends angels to announce important messages or to guide certain people at critical moments. When you think about it, the fact that this child was to be born of a virgin and destined to become the promised Messiah was a mind-boggling concept to accept. That had never happened before. God had to take special measures to communicate.

You'll also notice several references to Old Testament prophecies. As we discovered in earlier chapters of **EssentialJESUS**, God had given many clues – previews or trailers – that he was planning to send a Saviour to the world. The good news is that the time had finally come. No more previews; it was finally time for the main event. God entered the world in the person of his Son, Jesus.

Finally, it's fascinating to examine how all the different people in these next readings reacted to the coming of Jesus. Joseph and Mary, the shepherds and wise men, religious leaders and King Herod – all grappled with what was happening. Centuries later, we are able to appreciate more fully the truth as expressed in one of the names used to describe Jesus: Emmanuel, or 'God with us'. But don't take my word for it. You need to discover the true meaning of Christmas on your own. And that's what this next section is all about, Charlie Brown!

31   **Favour with God**

Date: *The birth of Jesus*

PRAY   'My soul glorifies the Lord and my spirit rejoices in God my Saviour, for he has been mindful of the humble state of his servant' (Luke 1:46–48).

READ   Luke 1:26–56

REFLECT

How would you feel if an angel appeared to you? I'd like to think I'd be cool and stand my ground; more than likely I'd just run. Mary was 'greatly troubled' and afraid, but at least she stayed and listened. Perhaps she sensed that this was a messenger from God.

Mary is one of the great heroines of the Bible, a fact the angel confirms in the most incredible way (1:30). How can we, like Mary, find favour with God today? Let's take a closer look at how Mary responded to this surprise visitor to see if we can find some clues.

First, we notice that she is *confident in her relationship to God*. She's not proud, nor falsely modest. She sees herself simply as 'the Lord's servant' (1:38). As followers of Jesus today, we too are favoured by God, not because of anything we've done but rather because of what he's done for us (Ephesians 2:8–10). Mary's experience demonstrates that God uses people who have a humble confidence in him.

Second, we notice her *willingness to live by faith* (1:38,45). She reminds us of another Bible hero, Abraham, who left everything to follow God's call (Genesis 12:1–9), a fact that reverberates throughout the Bible (Romans 4:3; Hebrews 11:8–12).

Finally, we notice her *heart for God* (1:46–55). Mary's song (often called the Magnificat) is filled with Old Testament imagery, indicating that she was a young woman who had spent time reflecting on the Scriptures. In Mary we see the value of being saturated in God's Word.

Our passage also contains one of the most popular verses in the Bible: 'For nothing is impossible with God' (1:37). Short and positive, it's sure to give us hope when life gets stressful. But, seen in its context, the verse actually shows us that God intervenes in the lives of people, like Mary, who have developed a lifestyle of faithfully seeking him.

APPLY   Having looked at Mary's character, what qualities would you say most suited her to be the mother of Jesus? Do you find any of these qualities in your own life?

PRAY   Lord, show me some practical ways I can draw closer to you today.

32

Just the facts

Date: *The birth of Jesus*

PRAY Lord God, as I read this passage in the Bible, please communicate something new about Jesus to me.

READ Matthew 1:18–25

REFLECT

You can tell this version of the birth of Jesus was written by an accountant (Matthew 10:3). Matthew began his Gospel with a genealogy (1:1–17) – not exactly a page-turner! Now he describes the most exciting event in the history of the world as if it's a footnote in a financial report: '... before they came together, she was found to be with child' (1:18). 'Hello–oooo! Is that all you can say?'

But we shouldn't dismiss Matthew's perspective for its lack of dramatic flair. He understood the most important thing: Jesus was born to save people from their sins (1:21). There's no need to put any spin on a fact like that.

People struggle with the idea of the virgin birth (1:20). After all, it's the twenty-first century. We know science. We know biology. We know that could never happen... right?

Just because something is beyond our understanding doesn't mean it isn't true. Notice that Matthew doesn't present the virgin birth as some easy-to-swallow fairy tale. Even Mary and Joseph had trouble grasping what was happening (Luke 1:34;19). But that realistic struggle with the facts leads to a stronger faith and gives the Bible what translator JB Phillips called 'the ring of truth'.

Perhaps the biggest fact to emerge from Matthew's report is that the birth of Jesus was no accident. It was all God's doing. As we see in this passage and several others related to Jesus' birth, God sent angels to explain his intentions and to direct the action when necessary. Not only that, as we discovered in our Old Testament readings, he had spoken through the prophets long before predicting that these events would occur (1:22,23).

Matthew's straightforward account of Jesus' birth leads us to one important conclusion: God is active in his world and communicates with his people. And that's a fact.

APPLY For you, what are the most important facts about Jesus coming to earth? Are there any with which you struggle?

PRAY Spend a few minutes thanking God for the things you know about Jesus. Then ask him to help you understand the things about Jesus that aren't so clear to you now.

33   **Blockbuster truth**

Date: *The birth of Jesus*

PRAY   Lord, the world seems out of control sometimes. But I'm
                so thankful to have the solid truth of your Word to give
                me perspective.

READ   Luke 2:1–40

REFLECT

If Matthew wrote like an accountant, Luke wrote like a screenwriter.
His account of the birth of Jesus captures the dramatic texture that
makes for a good movie: the harrowing night-time journey of the 'star'
couple (2:4–7); the comic relief of the confused shepherds (2:8–
12,16–20) and the grand spectacle of an angel choir (2:13,14). The
Bible shows us that God used different personalities and perspectives
to communicate many angles of the gospel truth.

I'm convinced that the most overlooked characters in this passage are
the shepherds, and yet they seemed to come to the deepest
understanding of what was really happening. Low down on the
economic totem pole of their day, shepherds weren't the kind of
people you'd expect God to speak to.

But it's how this unlikely supporting cast responded to the good news
that's so instructive to us today. Note that the shepherds weren't too
busy to investigate the claims about Jesus (2:15); they instinctively
realised that finding Jesus was important so they made it a priority
(2:16). Next, they didn't consider the truth about Jesus 'a private
thing'. Instead, they immediately began telling others what they had
discovered (2:17) and were unashamed to worship God enthusiast-
ically (2:20). Those are the marks of Jesus' true followers.

Our passage ends with cameo appearances by Simeon and Anna
(2:25–38). In a modern film, these scenes might have ended up on the
cutting-room floor. But Luke included them because they are an
important part of the story. God knew that the events surrounding the
birth of Jesus would seem unbelievable to Joseph, Mary and maybe
even to us. So he confirms what he was doing through these
prophecies. It reminds us that God has done everything he could
think of to let us know the truth about his Son.

APPLY   Which character in the story of Jesus' birth do you
                identify with the most? Why?

PRAY   Thank you, God, for going to such great lengths to
                communicate the truth about Jesus to me. Give me the
                courage to tell others the good news.

34   **Searching for Jesus**

The birth of Jesus

PRAY   Father God, as I read today please help me understand
             the truth about who your Son Jesus really is.

READ   Matthew 2:1–23

REFLECT

In 1985 a group of liberal scholars founded 'The Jesus Seminar',
supposedly to search for the real Jesus. Over the next decade, they
isolated 176 events in the life of Jesus as reported in the Gospels and
then voted using coloured beads on whether they thought each one
really happened. The result? The scholars concluded that only 16 per
cent of the events did or probably did happen. But these scholars have
been criticised over the years for their bias: after all, it's hard to find
the Son of God when you don't believe he exists!

In this passage, the Magi or Wise Men embarked on an honest search
for Jesus. They asked good questions, followed the evidence and
remained open to the possibility that Jesus was the Messiah (2:2). In
the end, they found and worshipped him (2:11,12). Herod's search,
on the other hand, was unsuccessful.

Another feature of this passage is the odyssey of Joseph and Mary.
Think about it. They knew God was at work on their behalf; they had
been visited by angels, shepherds and wise men. And they knew better
than anyone else about the miraculous circumstances of Jesus' birth.
Their boy was the promised Messiah. So it would be natural for them
to think that life would be safe and secure. Not so. God's plan was to
make them vulnerable refugees (2:13–15).

Sometimes being in the centre of God's will means our lives won't be
successful or easy; sometimes he needs us to travel the hard road. But
we can be sure that, no matter where he leads, God has a purpose in
mind (Romans 8:28). In this case, he was protecting this special
family (2:19,20) and in the process fulfilling the plan he had
announced centuries earlier (2:23). God always knows what he is
doing in our lives, even when his plan isn't so clear to us.

APPLY   Travelling with Jesus doesn't always guarantee an easy
             road. What have you learned from the hard roads in your
             life?

PRAY   Think of the most difficult situation you face today or
             this week. Spend some time asking Jesus to help you trust
             him for the outcome.

35

His Father's Son

The birth of Jesus

PRAY   Heavenly Father, sometimes my mind is racing with everything I have to do. I need to slow down... slow down... slow down... so I can hear what you have to say to me today.

READ   Luke 2:41–52

REFLECT

I know exactly how Joseph and Mary felt (2:48). I remember the time I lost track of our youngest daughter Stephanie in a department store. She was about five years old and after ten minutes of desperate searching I was going berserk. When I finally found her hiding and grinning in the middle of a rack of clothes, I felt a mixture of anger and relief.

But, as we see in this passage, Jesus wasn't playing 'hide-and-seek' in the Temple. He was beginning to demonstrate his unique nature. Even as a pre-teen he possessed amazing wisdom far beyond his years (2:47).

And notice how Jesus reacts to Mary's reference to 'your father' (2:48). I heard those words a few times growing up: 'When your father gets home... ' Without missing a beat, Jesus responds, 'Didn't you know that I had to be in my Father's house?' Jesus already understood that he was the divine Son of God. It wasn't a claim he invented later on to attract a crowd. He was born that way.

The interchange between Mary and Jesus also introduces us to a tension that builds throughout the Gospel accounts. Jesus often said things that assumed his divine nature and unique relationship to God. Some people missed his point or were confused by what he said. Other people clearly understood what Jesus meant and became angry or rejected him for it. That's how the religious leaders reacted to Jesus throughout his life. In fact, his words made them so angry over time that they finally killed him for it. I wonder if some of the leaders who chatted with Jesus in the Temple that day were present 21 years later when he was crucified?

APPLY   What are your favourite statements of Jesus? Are there things Jesus said that you find hard to accept?

PRAY   Lord Jesus, whether your words are encouraging or challenging, I ask for the ability to honestly hear what you are saying to me.

DISCUSSION QUESTIONS: THE BIRTH OF JESUS

After you've completed the five readings in this section, get together with another person or group to talk about the things you've learned. Begin by sharing the insights you gained from your own reflection on the passages. Then use the following questions to help you continue the conversation.

1   Throughout the account of Jesus' birth, God sent angels to announce the arrival and to direct the action. Why do you suppose he chose to do this?

2   When Jesus was born, the angel announced that it was 'good news'? What exactly is the 'good news'? Can you describe it in your own words?

3   Do you think most people know the real meaning of Christmas? How would you explain what Christmas is to your non-believing friends or colleagues?

4   Do you think people should lobby to have Jesus become more visible in Christmas decorations? What are some effective ways to put Christ into Christmas?

5   Have you ever had an experience that made no sense at the time but later convinced you that God was at work? What happened?

6   Why do you think Jesus' claim to be the Son of God makes some people angry?

THE BEGINNING MINISTRY OF JESUS

I once watched a television documentary about the life of popular singer Bob Dylan. It was fun to watch footage of the scruffy-haired star singing his greatest hits, including *Blowin' in the Wind*, *The Times They are A-Changin'*, *Like a Rollin' Stone* and many more. But the part of the programe that most interested me was his early career, especially the year when he made the transition from an unknown folk singer in Minnesota named Robert Zimmerman to a 'discovered' rock star in New York City named Bob Dylan.

Of course Jesus was far more than a rock star, but in our next five readings we'll be examining a similar transition period in his life, as he goes from being an unknown carpenter from Nazareth to a popular preacher and healer who attracted big crowds. Unfortunately, there's no television footage from those exciting days! But there is plenty of vivid detail captured in the Gospel accounts.

First, we'll look at what amounts to Jesus' public debut: his baptism. John the Baptist was creating quite a stir by preaching a tough message of repentance, and people were lining up to be 'washed' in the Jordan River to publicly mark a turning towards God. But when Jesus' turn came, God spoke loud and clear: 'This is my Son, whom I love; with him I am well pleased' (Matthew 3:17). From the very beginning it was clear that Jesus was more than a carpenter.

That's why the devil attacked him right away in the desert, as we'll see next. We sometimes think temptation comes when we do the wrong thing or allow ourselves to get into bad situations. That's often true enough. But temptation can also come when we are trying to do the right thing; Jesus was in the middle of a 40-day spiritual retreat. We'll learn how Jesus dealt with temptation – something that is incredibly helpful to know today.

Finally, as his ministry begins to pick up steam, we'll hear Jesus articulate his mission statement, we'll examine the nature of his ministry and we'll watch as he begins recruiting his team. It's all exciting stuff.

One key theme that emerged from the early days of Jesus' ministry was his commitment to finding followers. In fact, throughout the Gospel accounts we see Jesus giving the simple challenge: 'Follow me.' That little phrase was packed with a huge meaning, both for his original hearers and for us, as we're about to find out.

36   'This is my son... '

Date: *The beginning ministry of Jesus*

PRAY   'Praise be to the Lord, to God our Saviour, who daily bears our burdens' (Psalm 68:19). Spend some time putting your burdens before the Lord.

READ   Matthew 3

REFLECT

I wonder if John the Baptist was a fun person to be around. Think about it: he was a negative conversationalist (3:2) and had a knack for offending people (3:7). Not only that, he was a wierd dresser and had strange ideas about food (3:4). He probably had bad breath too. How could such an oddball become such a popular preacher (3:5)? The answer is simple: he had a unique twofold message that people were hungry to hear:

Repent! John told people they were sinners, and he told them what to do about it (3:8). You wouldn't think that would be such a popular theme. But, to people weighed down by sin, a call to repentance is a blessing. If you've ever been forgiven for something you've done wrong, you know what I'm talking about. Unconfessed sin has a way of eating us up from the inside out. But when we repent and finally get free of our guilt, we experience a sense of relief and joy. Perhaps those who think repentance is negative haven't tried it yet.

The kingdom of God is coming! John the Baptist was the first person to announce publicly the fact that his younger cousin Jesus was actually the Messiah (Luke 1:36) and was bringing in a new era of relationship with God. That took a lot of humility (3:11), but that was John's calling (3:3).

All of this set the stage for a milestone event in the Gospel narrative (3:13–17). Although John didn't understand, Jesus knew it was important for him to be baptised because it would become a unique demonstration of his divine nature. And how interesting that all three Persons of the Trinity were involved: the Son was baptised, the Holy Spirit descended, and the Father spoke.

APPLY   Which part of John the Baptist's message applies the most to you now? Do you need to hear about repentance? Or the nearness of Jesus? Why?

PRAY   Lord Jesus, there are lots of things I don't understand but I do want to get closer to you. Please show me the things that stand in the way of that.

37

Deliver us from evil

Date: *The beginning ministry of Jesus*

PRAY Heavenly Father, this world can be a dark and evil place at times. Please show me how I can be an instrument of your light.

READ Luke 4:1–13

REFLECT

Do you believe in the devil? I do. I've never had an encounter with him, nor do I want to. But I've seen the effect of the devil's work in the lives of broken and destroyed people. As we see in this passage, the devil was attempting to destroy Jesus in three ways:

The promise of granting physical desires There's nothing wrong with food or eating in moderation. But the devil attempts to use Jesus' hunger to make him forget who he really is. Note the taunt: '*If* you are the Son of God... ' (4:3). One of the devil's most effective strategies is to destroy people by causing them to take a natural desire to an evil extreme.

The promise of worldly power This is the classic 'making a deal with the devil' that has become the premise for so many plays and novels: 'If you worship me, it will all be yours' (4:7). Again, the drive to succeed is not wrong; taking it to the extreme is. Those who are successful need people who will hold them accountable. Note that power and fame are tools the devil claims as his own (4:6).

The promise of spiritual power The devil returns to his original taunt (4:3,9) but attaches it to a quotation from Psalm 91. Perhaps spiritual temptations are the most subtle and dangerous. The devil doesn't need to stop us from doing God's work as long as he can get us to be ungodly as we do it. That still advances his evil agenda.

Jesus didn't fall for any of the devil's tactics. In each case he used his knowledge of the Scriptures to repel the attack. And if Jesus needed God's Word to resist evil, we need it even more. Our struggle with temptation won't end (4:13) until God deals with the devil once and for all (Revelation 20:10).

APPLY To which kind of temptation are you most vulnerable? What's your strategy for resisting?

PRAY Use the prayer Jesus gave his followers (Matthew 6:9–15) as your outline for prayer now. Slowly say each phrase and add your own prayers to each.

38   Who does he think he is?

Date: *The beginning ministry of Jesus*

PRAY   'The grass withers and the flowers fall ... but the word of our God stands for ever' (Isaiah 40:7,8). Lord, open my eyes to something new from your eternal Word today.

READ   Luke 4:14–30

REFLECT

It must have been difficult to grow up around Jesus. The mums at the school gate no doubt talked for years about the details of Mary's pregnancy and her son's birth. As Jesus grew up, the religious teachers would have debated what this child prodigy was destined to become. And his 'church friends' must have been flabbergasted when Jesus stepped into the spotlight at the Temple that day. Everyone who knew Jesus would have been wondering the same thing: 'Who does he think he is?'

The answer to that basic question begins to emerge in this passage. When Jesus stood up and read from the book of Isaiah, he was indicating at least two very important things about himself:

He had a mission. Jesus was saying that he came 'to preach good news to the poor... ' (4:17–19). The Gospels help us understand that a person can be physically or spiritually poor (see Matthew 5:3 and Luke 6:20). Either way, Jesus had come for such as them.

He was more than just a man. Jesus was saying that he was more than a carpenter's son (4:22). You'll remember from one of our earlier readings that this passage in Isaiah was one of four places in that book which describe the coming Deliverer (the 'Servant Songs'). By saying this had been fulfilled (4:21), Jesus was clearly claiming he was that promised Messiah. You can imagine the stunned silence that followed: 'Ah, right... are there any other announcements today?'

Ever since, people have been divided about Jesus. Some accept him (4:22) while others are infuriated by him (4:28). And, as you'll see in the rest of our journey through the Bible, Jesus made many more jaw-dropping statements about what he came to do (for example, John 5:24–27). A person who said what Jesus said and did what Jesus did demands a response.

APPLY   If you had been in the Temple with Jesus that day, how do you think you would have reacted to his claim?

PRAY   In your own words, complete this prayer, 'Jesus, this is who I honestly think you are...'

39   With authority!

Date: *The beginning ministry of Jesus*

PRAY   In spite of the stresses and problems that are in my life right now, Lord, I'm eager to read your Word because I know you have something to say to me.

READ   Luke 4:31–44

REFLECT

As a result of my involvement in prison work, I became good friends with a man named Aaron Johnson, a Baptist minister who had been appointed as the Secretary of Correction in North Carolina. After taking the job, his first decision was to ban swearing and pornography in all state prisons. When his lieutenants questioned the practicality of what he proposed, Rev Johnson responded with a preacher's conviction: 'Do I have the *authority* to make this decision?' 'Well, yes. You do, Mr Secretary.' 'Fine! No more swearing or pornography in the prisons.'

Our passage today shows Jesus going public with his ministry. No longer is he just a local celebrity – he's starting to travel and attract crowds (4:31,43,44). And, as he does, the distinctive feature that is evident to all is his *authority*. We see it both in his teaching (4:32) and in his healing (4:36). We've already learned that Jesus was saturated in Scripture and empowered by the Spirit. No wonder he had such a dynamic ministry.

It's significant that the demon-possessed heckler met Jesus in the synagogue, not in the back alley. Today, we assume sometimes that churches are for 'good' people. But if the Church is doing its job, those who are disturbed or who have serious problems will also be attracted to the fellowship. Instead of rejecting or avoiding them, we need to introduce them to Jesus; he's the one with the authority to change their lives (4:35).

Our passage gives us one other clue about the source of Jesus' authority: 'At daybreak Jesus went out to a solitary place.' In the hustle and bustle of his growing popularity, Jesus made time to be alone with God in prayer. Even though he was the Son of God, he made it a priority to talk with his Father. And that's a source of strength that's still available to us today.

APPLY   Imagine what it would have been like to be in the crowd listening to Jesus. How would you have felt? What would you have done?

PRAY   Following the example of Jesus, try to spend some time alone with God today, getting to know him better.

40   Jesus' leadership style

Date: *The beginning ministry of Jesus*

PRAY   Father, I ask for a clearer picture of who you are as I read your Word today.

READ   Luke 5:1–11

REFLECT

In the book *The Future of the Leader*, business expert Peter Drucker makes this deceptively profound statement: 'A leader is someone who has followers.' His point is simply this: regardless of your title or what you wear or how you talk, regardless of management theory, if you can't motivate people to follow you, you're not a leader. In our passage today, we get a unique insight into how the world's greatest leader recruited followers.

He shared God's Word with people. The crowds were attracted to Jesus not because he was a showman, but rather because he was sharing the Word of God (5:1). That's still the key to church growth. As we read through the Gospels, we see that Jesus often baffled people by doing the opposite of what they thought would gain popularity (John 6:60,66). But Jesus' goal was not popularity; it was to attract followers (Matthew 9:9; Mark 1:17; Luke 18:22; John 21:19).

He spoke to people individually and in a language they understood. Jesus recruited followers one at a time. Look at Peter's experience (5:4–11). Jesus took the trouble to communicate in a 'language' Peter could understand: the fishing business. We make a mistake if we think that God only works in a church or other religious setting. God is at work everywhere in his world. Life takes on new meaning when we look for him in the details of our day.

His presence convicted people of their need for God. The bulging nets convinced Peter he was in the presence of a higher power (5:8). Interestingly, his first thought wasn't to snap a picture for the wall of his den: Peter and Jesus, arm in arm, in front of the unbelievable mound of fish. Instead, he thought of his sin. That's what a real encounter with God does. It reveals the distance between God's holiness and our corruption. Even so, we have nothing to fear (5:10). Jesus came to restore the relationship between sinful humans and a holy God. That's the reason to follow him.

APPLY   Do you ever feel afraid of God? Why?

PRAY   Jesus, open my eyes to the ways that you are at work in the details of my day and life.

DISCUSSION QUESTIONS: THE BEGINNING MINISTRY OF JESUS

After you've completed the five readings in this section, get together with another person or group to talk about the things you've learned. Begin by sharing the insights you gained from your own reflection on the passages. Then use the following questions to help you continue the conversation.

1   Do you think that God is pleased with you (Matthew 3:17)? Why? Or why not?

2   Jesus spent 40 days in the wilderness. Why do you think he needed to be alone with God? Do you have that same need? How do you spend time alone with God?

3   Jesus was tempted by the devil. How could you summarise his response and how might that help you when you are tempted?

4   Looking at the example of Jesus here, what do you think about his use of fasting and praying? Have you any personal experience of the benefits of these spiritual exercises?

5   Does the church you attend attract people who are disturbed or troubled? How could your congregation be more effective at introducing these and all people to Jesus?

6   Jesus challenged his followers to 'Come, follow me... and I will send you out to fish for people' (Matthew 4:19, TNIV). What do you think he meant? How can anyone 'fish for people' today?

THE SERMONS OF JESUS

How many sermons have you listened to in your lifetime? Probably too many to count. I'm sure I've heard thousands, but I don't know if I'll ever apply even half what I've heard. There's one thing, however, that I know for sure. I'd trade all the sermons I've ever heard just to listen to *one* from Jesus. In our next five readings we'll have the privilege of reading three major sermons of Jesus found in the Gospels.

The Sermon on the Mount (Matthew 5–7) is undoubtedly the most famous sermon ever preached. Jesus delivered it at the beginning of his public ministry and used it to spell out his view of the world. What we notice right away is that Jesus' worldview and our worldview are radically different. He starts with what has become known as 'the Beatitudes', a series of statements that might seem like devotional inspirations, until you actually think about what he's saying. Jesus wants his followers to be poor in spirit, meek, hungry for righteousness, merciful, pure in heart, committed to peacemaking and willing to endure persecution for living that way. Hmmm…

He goes on to set some more incredibly high standards for his followers: we should love our enemies, help the needy, stop worrying about money and make his kingdom our first priority. In fact, at one point, he even says, 'Be perfect, therefore, as your heavenly Father is perfect' (Matthew 5:48). Wow!

In the next sermon, we'll discover a hard edge to Jesus' preaching, which may come as a surprise. In his 'Seven Woes' sermon, Jesus lays into the religious leaders of the day, relentlessly pounding them for not practising what they preached. But, even in the midst of this angry tongue-lashing, Jesus never stops loving his listeners. As he says at the end, 'How often I have longed to gather your children together, as a hen gathers her chicks under her wings, but you were not willing' (Matthew 23:37).

In the final sermon we'll cover in this section, Jesus boldly predicts the end of the religious establishment of his day and then bridges to a description of the end of the world. It's spellbinding.

So hold onto your seat. You're about to listen to the words of the world's greatest preacher…

41 The 'new' reality

Date: *The sermons of Jesus*

PRAY   Lord God, help me to come to the words of Jesus as if I'm hearing them for the first time.

READ   Matthew 5

REFLECT

What we call the Sermon on the Mount has become the most famous sermon of all time. Some people think it's just a collection of little moral or 'blessed' statements. But a careful look reveals that Jesus preached about a large and challenging topic: the kingdom of heaven (referred to elsewhere in the Gospels as the kingdom of God). What exactly is it?

In general, the kingdom of heaven refers to God's rule on the earth. That's what Jesus came to announce and establish. And this involves two distinct realities.

The internal reality Those who belong to the kingdom of heaven have a heart that is committed to the values that are important to God; they are humble, meek, merciful, peace-loving, righteous, pure and so on (5:3–10). Jesus says people like that will be rewarded by God (5:12). They will also be persecuted (5:11) because those who live out God's values will challenge the darkness and corruption of the world (5:13–16).

The external reality Throughout the Old Testament, God's people were instructed to obey God's laws or suffer the consequences. That led to a system of legalism: just do the right thing and you're good with God. But note how Jesus repeats the phrase, 'You have heard that it was said… '. He's holding up various Old Testament laws and linking them to the new motivation of the kingdom of heaven. In essence he's saying, 'It's not good enough simply to do the right thing; you need to do it for the right reason.'

A new inner reality and a new external reality – that's what it means to belong to this new kingdom. That's what God had in mind all along (5:17–20).

APPLY   What challenges you most from the words of Jesus in this passage?

PRAY   Which of the things mentioned in verses 3–10 would you like to see more of in your life? Make that the focus of your prayers to Jesus.

42   Hungry for God

The sermons of Jesus

PRAY   Father, I want to draw closer to you today in spite of the
             worries and pressures on me right now. Please lift them
             so I can sense your presence.

READ   Matthew 6

REFLECT

I remember the first time I read *Celebration of Discipline*, Richard
Foster's classic book about spiritual disciplines. I was eating lunch by
myself in a MacDonald's restaurant in downtown Philadelphia and
was so moved tears came to my eyes. I didn't realise it at the time – but
I was hungry for more than a Big Mac. I wanted a deeper relationship
with God, and Foster was describing a way to find it that was new for
me.

I should have read the Sermon on the Mount too on that day, because
that's exactly the topic Jesus addresses in this part of it: spiritual
disciplines. He starts by discussing three that you would expect him to
cover:

About giving (6:1–4) – he says it shouldn't be done for PR value;
rather, we should keep a low profile.

About prayer (6:5–15) – he says the focus should be spending time
alone with God.

About fasting (6:16–18) – he says we shouldn't act like holier-than-
thou martyrs.

Jesus concludes this section with two unexpected topics: *money* (6:19–
24) and *worry* (6:25–34). We don't usually think of these as spiritual
issues but they often keep us from drawing closer to God. For me,
worry is the bigger issue. I worry about our children, my work, my
health and the future. Sometimes I act as if it's responsible to worry.
But worry is emotionally and spiritually exhausting. That's why it
helps to return again and again to the greatest spiritual discipline of
all: seek first his kingdom and his righteousness (6:33). That puts
everything else into its proper perspective.

APPLY   How do you respond to Jesus' challenges here about the
             priorities of your life?

PRAY   Talk to God about the hold of money and worry in your
             life. Ask him to show you how to give his kingdom first
             place.

43   The great communicator

Date: *The sermons of Jesus*

PRAY   Father, you know better than anyone what I need to hear right now. Please help me be open to a special communication from you in this passage.

READ   Matthew 7

REFLECT

Jesus broke all the rules for effective communicators. The Sermon on the Mount was long (needing much more than the average attention span of 15 minutes!), delivered outside without a sound system and included no jokes – not even a funny story! But Jesus amazed the crowds because he had the one thing no communication coach could ever teach: authority (7:29). The Son of God was able to communicate the Word of God like no one else could.

In the last part of the Sermon on the Mount, Jesus zeroes in on three main points.

Judging others: don't do it! Christians must walk a fine line on this issue; on the one hand they must hate sin but, on the other, they must love the sinner. Easier said than done. Perhaps that's why Jesus suggested that we focus on removing our own sins; if we do, there won't be much time for anything else.

Seeking God: do it! Some people seem to have an 'entitlement mentality' when it comes to God; they think he owes them something whether they believe in him or not. But Jesus counsels a proactive approach to finding God (7:7,8): God blesses those who sincerely seek him (7:9–11; see also Hebrews 11:6).

False prophets: watch out! Our world is full of religious gurus who seem good but in fact are dangerous (7:15); following the wrong one can have serious consequences (7:22,23). To prevent this, we first need to evaluate the actions ('fruit', 7:16) of any teacher. Next we need to determine if their message is consistent with God's will, which for us is most clearly expressed in the Bible.

Jesus wraps up the world's greatest sermon with a straightforward analogy about houses built on sand and rock. The point? Build your life on the rock-solid words of Jesus. Nothing complicated about that.

APPLY   Do you feel confident enough in the words of Jesus to make them foundational in your life?

PRAY   Jesus, I want to take your advice to heart. Help me not to judge others, but to seek God and beware of wrong teaching.

44

No more Mr Nice Guy

Date: *The sermons of Jesus*

PRAY   Heavenly Father, I love having your Word as a reference point. Please guide me through what I read today.

READ   Matthew 23

REFLECT

Niccolo Machiavelli (1469–1527) was an Italian political thinker who gained lasting notoriety for, among other things, his 'end justifies the means' philosophy and his dislike of Christianity. In Machiavelli's view, Jesus was so humble and meek he could never make an impact in the 'real world'.

But perhaps Machiavelli should have studied this passage. In it, he would encounter a passionate, angry Jesus who had no trouble getting in the face of his opponents when necessary. It's a misconception to think that being a Christian means you have to act like a wimp. Biblical characters are often encouraged to become 'strong and courageous' (Joshua 1:7). The key, however, is to be sure we are pursuing God's agenda, not our own, when we do.

So what got Jesus so angry? The answer boils down to a single word: *hypocrisy*. The teachers of the Law and the Pharisees – the religious leaders at the time – weren't practising what they preached (23:3). Notice the strong language Jesus used: blind guides (23:16), blind fools (23:17), snakes, brood of vipers (23:33). No one likes a hypocrite.

In fact, the tension between Jesus and these leaders had been building for a long time (Luke 4:28–30; 6:11). In the previous chapter they tried to trap and discredit Jesus (22:15,18). Even though they seemed like holy men, their motives were clear to Jesus (Matthew 12:14). True holiness doesn't come from a fancy religious title or from acting in a saintly way. There are many things we can do to *appear* holy, but that's all it is: appearance. True holiness requires complete harmony between God's priorities and our actions (23:23).

Machiavelli thought that strong people were those who ruthlessly did whatever necessary to maintain power and authority, even if it meant lying and deception. Jesus demonstrated that true strength involves standing up for God's agenda, no matter what the circumstances.

APPLY   Is there a situation in your life that will require you to stand up for God's agenda? How will you do this?

PRAY   Jesus, help me to experience your strength and courage in the challenges I face today.

45

The end

Date:

PRAY   Lord, please help me see the world and my life from your
perspective as I read your Word today.

READ   Matthew 24

REFLECT

Jesus got into big trouble for his little sound bite about the Temple
(24:1,2); it seemed as if he was planning a terrorist attack on the most
revered structure in all of Judaism. Although there's no direct
comparison today, it would be something like someone claiming the
intention to blow up Buckingham Palace, Westminster Abbey and St
Paul's Cathedral all at once.

But Jesus wasn't really talking about a physical building, he was
talking about his 'body' – the Church or, in other words, all those who
would believe and follow him (John 2:19–22). That's what would
replace the stone Temple, impressive though it was. The disciples had
trouble grasping all that (24:3) so later Jesus took time to explain,
which is what the main part of our reading is all about.

An examination of what Jesus said in this private sermon reveals that
he had at least three perspectives in mind.

He was predicting the Temple would eventually be destroyed (24:2). But he
wouldn't be the one to do it, he said. As it turned out, the Roman
legions took care of that when they burned it to the ground in AD 70.
Jesus was counselling us not to put our faith in bricks and mortar or
anything else in this world; it's all temporary.

He was predicting his disciples were in for some tough times (24:4–14).
Jesus' followers would be 'persecuted ... put to death ... hated'. Soon
after Jesus' death and resurrection, that's exactly what happened. His
followers were persecuted, first by the Jews (Acts 8:1–3) and then by
the Romans. Jesus was warning us too that following him won't always
be a bed of roses.

He was predicting the end of the world (24:15–51). This will be a time of
great stress and worldwide tumult; some say it has begun to happen
today. But the followers of Christ have nothing to fear because,
regardless of what happens or when it does, the most important thing
is that Jesus will one day return. Jesus was advising us to be ready and
waiting for that day (24:44).

APPLY   Are you ready for the return of Jesus?

PRAY   Father in heaven, I ask that you help me focus more on
what is eternal and less on what is temporary in my life.

DISCUSSION QUESTIONS: THE SERMONS OF JESUS

After you've completed the five readings in this section, get together with another person or group to talk about the things you've learned. Begin by sharing the insights you gained from your own reflection on the passages. Then use the following questions to help you continue the conversation.

1   What do you think of Jesus' teaching in the Beatitudes (Matthew 5:1–12)? Is this just a collection of ideals? Or do you think we should really try to live that way today?

2   What do you know about Jesus' experiences of being insulted and persecuted? How practical do you think his advice about being on the receiving end of such treatment really is?

3   Jesus said, 'Do not worry about your life...' (Matthew 6:25). Talk about how you're doing with that challenge.

4   Think about Jesus' challenges on priorities. Which has a greater hold on your life – God or money? What's your evidence?

5   What do you think about Jesus' criticism of the religious leaders of his day? Do you think church leaders today are hypocrites? What would Jesus say to the church leaders you know?

6   How does the fact that the world will end and Jesus will return some day affect your life and decisions?

THE PARABLES OF JESUS

I used to give children's talks at our church in Philadelphia. In the middle of the service, all the kids in the congregation were invited to the front rows. My job was to deliver a three- to five-minute talk that captured the essence of what our pastor would later preach to the grown ups.

The first few times didn't go too well. The kids wriggled and giggled and didn't listen to anything I had to say. That's because I was boring; I simply told them what they were supposed to do: 'Be good. Always obey your parents. Blah, blah, blah.'

Then one Sunday I told the children a story. It described how I had done something wrong when I was a child, and what I learned from it. They loved it and gave me their full attention! So the next time I did the children's talk, I told another story – with similar results. Pretty soon that's all I did: tell stories about naughty little Whitney.

After a while I noticed something else. The adults liked my stories too! They'd come up to me during the coffee break to talk about what I'd said and to tell me their own stories. One time, a church elder told me, 'You know, Whitney, you've become quite the raconteur.' I had no idea what a raconteur was; all I knew was he liked my stories.

As you'll see in our next five readings, Jesus used stories – or parables – all the time in his ministry. In fact, judging from the material recorded in the four Gospels, he spent more time telling stories than he did preaching. Sometimes this teaching style perplexed his disciples; they once asked him bluntly, 'Why do you speak to the people in parables?' (Matthew 13:10).

He did it first of all because stories communicate; and second because he was speaking to such a wide variety of people. Some of his listeners were devoted followers, some were arch enemies, some were confused onlookers, some were hurting souls and some, like us, would only read his words centuries later. But all of them could relate to a good story.

So get ready. You are about to explore the parables of Jesus, the world's greatest storyteller.

46

Date:

Have mercy!

The parables of Jesus

PRAY   Father God, my heart's desire is to understand and experience you more today. Please help me do that as I think from your Word today.

READ   Luke 10:25–37

REFLECT

Recently I attended a discussion with an expert on global climate change. Although I'm convinced this is a very serious issue, I left early because many in the audience actually weren't interested in hearing what the scientist had to say. Instead, they wanted to draw attention to themselves by asking smart-sounding questions.

That's the challenge Jesus faced in this impromptu Q&A session. Initially, the expert in the Law wasn't interested in spiritual things, his intent was 'to test Jesus' (10:25). Even so, Jesus allowed him his 15 seconds of fame; I imagine the tone of verse 26 to be something like this: 'Okay, Mr Smarty Pants, why don't you show everyone how well you know the Scriptures?' But Jesus knew that beneath the man's desire to show off was a deeper need; he wasn't sure of his relationship with God (10:29).

Perhaps the expert was retreating to safer theological ground with his follow-up question about neighbours. But Jesus' goal was not to debate theology; it was to show us what God is like. In this situation he does so by telling a wonderful story we call The Good Samaritan (10:30–35). In it, the Levite and the priest (both religious experts of the time) failed to do what the Scriptures taught or what God wanted. In contrast, the Samaritan (the mixed-race outcast of the time) obeyed the Scriptures and pleased God.

The point is that if you want to know God you need to have mercy. Why? Because having mercy is the reason God sent his Son to earth. Like the Good Samaritan, Jesus went out of his way to find us. Like the Good Samaritan, Jesus paid the price to restore us. And like the Good Samaritan, Jesus made an enormous sacrifice to save us.

In spite of his impressive theological knowledge, the expert in the Law didn't have a clue about God's mercy. Ultimately, the best way for us to do that is to understand what happened on the cross.

APPLY   What does your understanding of Jesus tell you about mercy?

PRAY   Father, having mercy sounds good... but it's difficult to live out. Please help me practise mercy in my responses to people around me this week.

47

Rich towards God

Date: *The parables of Jesus*

PRAY Father, more than anything else, my goal is to have a deeper relationship with you. Please show me how I can do that today.

READ Luke 12:13–21

REFLECT

Talk about cheek! This man had the guts to interrupt Jesus in front of 'many thousands' (12:1) with a complaint about the family finances (12:13). You can almost hear the frustration in Jesus' voice. But before we come down too hard on this poor man, we need to ask if *our* money and possessions have ever caused us to lose sight of the more important things in life. No comment.

So what did Jesus say to this man and other distracted followers like us about money and possession?

Jesus puts his finger on the root problem of greed (12:15). Years later, the great teacher Paul said the same thing: 'For the love of money is the root of all kinds of evil' (1 Timothy 6:10). It's true that we need resources in order to survive. But Jesus warned that they can easily pull our hearts over the edge into greed, so we need to watch out.

Jesus reminds us that life is more than possessions (12:15). I'll say 'Amen' to that every time, but honestly I find it's easier said than done. On Saturday mornings, I love drinking a cup of coffee while looking at the glossy advertising inserts in the weekend paper. The funny thing is, when I'm done I often get this overwhelming urge to go buy something... anything! I know life is more than possessions, but...

Jesus illustrates his teaching with a story about a rich fool (12:20). This could be summarised like this: he who dies with the most toys... still dies. Notice that it wasn't the man who produced the incredible wealth for himself. Rather, the ground produced it (12:16). Jesus' point is very clear: even our ability to produce wealth is a gift from God. It all belongs to him. Our goal in life should not be to amass great wealth for ourselves. Rather, we should focus on becoming 'rich towards God' (12:21) and that will require us 'to do good, to be rich in good deeds, and to be generous and willing to share' (1 Timothy 6:18).

APPLY How do you respond to the challenges Jesus makes about material possessions?

PRAY God, thank you for the many material blessings you've given to me. Please show me how I can live a life that's rich towards you.

48   Happy meal

Date: *The parables of Jesus*

PRAY   Please help me be aware of your presence as I read, reflect, pray…

READ   Luke 14:1–24

REFLECT

It's difficult to understand Jesus' parable about a great banquet (14:16–24) without first appreciating the tense situation he was in when he told it: a dinner party with an influential group of his enemies.

Let's not miss the fact that Jesus engaged with those who didn't agree with him; he ate with them and prayed for them (Matthew 5:44). But he also got angry with them for caring more about their petty rules than for a needy person. When dos and don'ts become more important to us than showing compassion, we've lost touch with God's priorities, no matter how correct our rules may be. Religion based only on 'being right' looks good on the outside but leads to pride on the inside (14:7).

In the midst of the tension, someone blurts out a holy-sounding statement about a feast in the kingdom of God (14:15), perhaps thinking this 'happy meal' was a wonderful example of what it will be like. Jesus responds with a parable that makes one thing clear: the kingdom of God will be nothing like this tense, exclusive dinner party.

So what does Jesus teach about the kingdom of God from this parable?

God's intent is for all people to get into his kingdom. The banquet host goes to extraordinary lengths to make it possible for everyone to attend (14:17,21,23).

God's kingdom is not just for the wealthy and talented or those who have got their act together. The host also makes a special effort to include the down-and-outs: 'the poor, the crippled, the blind and the lame' (14:21).

It's possible to reject God's invitation. The fictional excuses (14:18–20,24) may sound silly, but they communicate an important truth: there's never a good reason for rejecting God's invitation.

Some day, God will host a great banquet for all those who have chosen to follow Jesus. What a happy meal that will be!

APPLY   How can you, like Jesus, take the initiative to engage with people who think differently to you?

PRAY   Thank you, Jesus, for that great banquet you're planning for your followers.

49   Sinners welcome!

Date: *The parables of Jesus*

PRAY   Lord, please show me anything that stands in the way of me drawing close to you.

READ   Luke 15

REFLECT

My church is located on a very busy road. Because of that, we've put up a huge sign above the main entrance that says 'Welcome!' We want to attract as many people as we can to worship with us. But, after reading today's passage, I wonder if we should change the sign to say, 'Sinners Welcome!' I wonder if it would attract more or fewer people?

However, I'm sure that Jesus would love the change because sinners were the focus of his ministry, a point that confounded the religious leaders (15:2). They thought religion should be reserved only for 'good' people like themselves. But Jesus demonstrated that true religion was for 'bad' people; and that all of us are sinners (Romans 3:23). That's a tough nut for anyone to swallow – so Jesus told three parables to explain what he meant.

The first two, about *a lost coin* and *a lost sheep* (15:3–10), are fairly straightforward. If you've ever misplaced a large amount of cash or lost a beloved pet, you can understand the feelings Jesus is describing. That's a picture of how God feels about sinners. He knows they're lost and he really wants to find them. That's good news for us.

The third parable, about *the prodigal (wasteful) son* (15:11–32), is more personal and adds a plot twist: sin. The younger brother wilfully does all the wrong things and deserves to be punished. As he blubbers on with a rehearsed apology, the suspense builds as to how the father will react. Will it be the cold shoulder, an angry tongue lashing, or complete rejection? It's none of the above. The father responds with joy over a sinner who has come home (15:22–24). In fact, the theme that unites the three parables is joy (15:6,7,9,23); God rejoices when sinners repent (15:7,10). That's even more good news.

But there's a catch. To experience that joyful reunion with God, you've got to admit that without him you're lost. You've must come to grips with your own sin. That's something the older brother (and the religious leaders, too) were unwilling to do (15:25–30). But it's the necessary first step to a relationship with God.

APPLY   With which of Jesus' characters can you identify more: the younger or the older brother? Why?

PRAY   Father, thank you that you are willing to welcome me back with open arms.

50

Uncommon prayer

Date: *The parables of Jesus*

PRAY   Lord Jesus, you took time to teach your disciples to pray. Help me better understand how to communicate with you.

READ   Luke 18:1–14

REFLECT

When I was in high school I loved English class (well, most of the time) because we got to study short stories. I enjoyed seeing how great authors could develop memorable characters and interesting plots in just a few pages. That's exactly what Jesus does in the two parables we read today.

Directed at followers The first one, about the persistent widow (18:1–8), was directed at the disciples and anyone else who wants to follow Jesus. There's a bit of humour in the interplay between the corrupt judge and the pestering woman. The surprising thing is that Jesus held this tireless agitator up as a model prayer warrior. But effective prayer doesn't always sound as if it comes from the *Book of Common Prayer.* Often it involves insisting, pleading and begging with God. It's important to note, however, that the woman's cause is consistent with God's priorities; she's praying for justice (18:3), not a new BMW.

Directed at the proud The second parable, about the Pharisee and the tax collector (18:9–14), was directed towards the proud and condescending (18:9). The obvious point is that God responds to the prayers of humility, not pride. The tricky thing is to know the difference, and that's not always easy. Getting involved in church, avoiding sin, pursuing spiritual disciplines are all good things... unless they cause us to look down on others. Prayers based on our own goodness don't get too far with God. Prayers based on our need for him get a much better reception.

Maybe these parables are less like a collection of short stories and more like another volume on my shelf at home. It's called *The Book of Uncommon Prayer* and it contains a collection of unorthodox but honest prayers through the ages. Jesus seems to be saying that, whatever they sound like, those are the ones God likes best.

APPLY   Is persistence in following Jesus difficult for you? Think about why that might be.

PRAY   Take a few minutes to say or even write out your own honest 'uncommon prayer'.

DISCUSSION QUESTIONS: THE PARABLES OF JESUS

After you've completed the five readings in this section, get together with another person or group to talk about the things you've learned. Begin by sharing the insights you gained from your own reflection on the passages. Then use the following questions to help you continue the conversation.

1 What have you learned from the Bible readings about Jesus and mercy? And compassion? Some people think that showing mercy is a sign of weakness. What do you think?

2 Do you have a personal philosophy about money and possessions? How does it compare with the teaching of Jesus as shown in his parables? Is it really possible to be wealthy but not 'possessed by possessions'?

3 Are you using the resources God has given you for maximum return – according to his priorities?

4 Revisit Jesus' story about the wasteful son (Luke 15:11–32). Was there ever a time in your life when you felt lost, far from God? What was it like? Have you made your way back to him yet? If so, how did it happen?

5 How has Jesus' story about the Pharisee and the tax collector (Luke 18:9–14) thrown light onto your understanding of pride? When is pride a good thing? And when is it bad? How do you know the difference?

MORE PARABLES OF JESUS

As we discovered in our last five readings, Jesus used parables all the time in his teaching ministry. He'd tell an interesting story to communicate an important or sometimes threatening truth to his listeners.

In our next five readings, we'll cover another set of parables based on two topics. The first is perhaps the greatest theme that emerges from Jesus' parables: the kingdom of heaven. We've already established a basic definition of that mysterious phrase: God's rule on the earth (see reading 41). But maybe that sounds too much like a quote from a theology book. We'll understand it much better when we read the stories Jesus told.

When you do, you'll notice that Jesus never said, 'The kingdom of heaven is this... full stop!' Instead, he said, 'The kingdom of heaven is *like...* ' and then he connected it to a good short story. That's because there is so much to understand. Each of the ten parables about the kingdom of heaven (some are very short so we'll read several at a time) gives us a different insight into this major theme. At the end, you'll need to piece everything together. It's like assembling a jigsaw puzzle; after a while you can begin to see the full picture (oops ... was that a parable?).

The second topic in this section is actually a variation of the parable teaching method. Jesus called it a 'figure of speech' (John 10:6). Instead of telling a full-blown story with a plot and a punchline, he pointed his listeners to a familiar object – a shepherd, a flock of sheep, a gate, a vine, some branches, a gardener – and used the analogy or comparison to explain significant truth.

Whether it's a story or a figure of speech, there's a lot to learn from the parables of Jesus. So let's get to it...

51

Date: *More parables of Jesus*

PRAY   Lord, you know the clutter that fills my heart and mind today. Please enable me to look beyond that to what you want me to see in your Word.

READ   Matthew 13

REFLECT

As we sort through this collection of six parables, it will help to remember our basic definition of the kingdom of heaven, since that's the theme which holds this chapter together. In essence, the kingdom of heaven is God's rule on the earth or, put another way, his territory and his people (see reading 41).

Perhaps the most famous of these parables is the first, about the sower. Jesus' description of a solitary farmer spreading seed by hand has been the subject of great paintings by Jean-François Millet (1851), Vincent van Gogh (1888) and many others. And even though most of us don't live in farming societies today, Jesus' reflections on where the seed fell still communicate an important truth about the Word of God: it must be received and nurtured in order to bear fruit in our lives.

Taken together, these parables help us see a more complete picture of the kingdom of heaven:

It starts small (like seeds); it has unique power to grow (like a mustard seed or yeast); it's worth everything you have (like hidden treasure or a pearl) and eventually it will include many, many people (like a net).

It's amazing how much truth Jesus packed into a few word sketches. But this raises an interesting question. Why did Jesus rely so much on parables (13:10)? The answer has to do with our willingness to receive his message. To learn from Jesus' parables requires that we receive his message with humility and faith – something many of his listeners lacked (13:58). By quoting from Isaiah (13:14,15) Jesus is saying that those who understand with their heads only – that is, without believing – don't really understand it at all. To enter the kingdom of heaven requires trust. That's what it means to 'understand with your heart' (13:15).

APPLY   What word picture would *you* use to describe your understanding of the kingdom of heaven? It's like...

PRAY   Jesus, I do want to be included in your kingdom. Please increase my knowledge and strengthen my belief in who you are and what you offer me.

52   The generous landowner

Date: *More parables of Jesus*

PRAY   Lord God, help me make my relationship with you more real and vital.

READ   Matthew 20:1–16

REFLECT

The punchline of this parable is familiar to most people (20:16). You might hear it quoted as a joke when someone queue jumps: 'Well, you know... the last will be first, and the first will be last.' But the parable and its punchline were no joke to Jesus. Through them he was communicating another important point about the kingdom of heaven. What did he have in mind?

The parable seems easy to understand at first: workers are hired at different points throughout the day with the promise of fair wages at the end. The suspense builds as the early birds anticipate how much overtime pay they might collect. But that's where the plot gets complicated; everyone receives the same amount. Those who worked 12 hours are paid the same as those who worked one hour. Now we are really confused. Is the landowner fair or unfair? Is he a rich oppressor or a heartless communist?

But Jesus is using this seeming unfairness to make a point. The kingdom of heaven cannot be earned; it's a gift from God (Ephesians 2:8,9). Instead of calling this 'the parable of the workers in the vineyard', it might be more accurate to call it 'the parable of the generous landowner' (20:15). Our salvation is dependent on God's generosity – not on our good works.

That was a tough message for the religious do-gooders of Jesus' day to accept. If anyone deserved to get into the kingdom of heaven, it was them – so they thought. But religion based on human effort and earning salvation leads away from God and into pride.

The truth is, God wants everyone to enjoy the benefits of his kingdom. Instead of grumbling about who deserves to be in or out (20:11,12) the workers would have done better to celebrate the generosity of the landowner. That's what it will be like in the kingdom of heaven.

APPLY   Thinking of Jesus' descriptions of the kingdom, which image best describes *your* view of the Christian faith: a rule book or a Christmas gift?

PRAY   Jesus, I can never repay you for what you did on the cross to open the way to your kingdom, but I am very, very grateful.

53

I wanna be ready!

Date: *More parables of Jesus*

PRAY   Before you read this chapter, take a minute to reflect
             prayerfully on 1 John 4:15–18.

READ   Matthew 25

REFLECT

I like parables that make a spiritual point with an everyday example. I
especially like it when Jesus slips in a clever little dig at the religious
leaders of his day. But this chapter makes *me* squirm. Darkness,
weeping, gnashing of teeth and eternal punishment (25:30,46)...
these parables are definitely not bedtime reading. What's got into
Jesus?

Actually, he's just completing his picture of the kingdom of heaven
(25:1,14). In earlier parables, Jesus made the point that God invites
everyone to enter his kingdom. But now he says some won't accept
that invitation; some will be left out and it won't be God's fault. The
ten virgins all had an opportunity to get ready for the bridegroom; five
used it wisely and five let it slip away (25:1–13). All three of the
servants received an investment from the wealthy man; two made the
most of it and one misused it (25:14–30).

The last parable is perhaps the most sobering of all (25:31–46). It
pictures a final day of reckoning where the Son of Man will sort out
the sheep from the goats; that is, he'll determine who will enter the
kingdom of heaven and who will not.

At first reading it might seem as if Jesus is saying we *can* earn our
salvation after all, if we just help the homeless, hungry, imprisoned
and needy. But we can't see this parable in isolation from his earlier
teaching. First, we must accept and believe in Jesus – that is, we must
'understand with our hearts' (Matthew 13:15). Then we must
demonstrate the reality of that belief through our compassionate
actions. It's the same thing the apostle James said many years later
(James 2:26).

Some people find the idea of a final judgement difficult to accept; they
feel that 'hellfire and brimstone' preaching is manipulative. Unfortunately, it can be. But that doesn't eliminate the reality that Jesus
will someday return to judge humankind. And no matter how we may
feel about it, the best response is this: use your time now to get ready.
Then you'll hear God say, 'Well done, good and faithful servant.'

APPLY   How do you feel about what Jesus is saying about a final
             day of judgement?

PRAY   Lord, sometimes the idea of judgement makes me fearful.
             Please reassure me with a deeper sense of your love today.

54

One way

Date:

More parables of Jesus

PRAY   Father, I long to hear your voice. Please help me listen
with my heart as I spend time with you and your Word.

READ   John 10:1–18

REFLECT

At different points in his teaching ministry, Jesus used a variation of
the parable style of teaching to communicate with his listeners. He
called it a 'figure of speech' (10:6). Instead of telling a story, he
presented word pictures or analogies and then used them to describe
several nuances of a spiritual truth. In our reading today, we find two
of these – the gate to a sheep pen and the good shepherd.

The gate The point of the gate picture is straightforward: Jesus is the
entry point into God's kingdom (10:9). I once taught a Sunday
School class for boys; they had trouble sitting still but asked lots of
good questions about Jesus. Sometime later, two parents publicly
criticised me for 'imposing' my belief that Jesus is the only way to
salvation on the class. My response was this: 'I'm sorry, but that's not
just my belief; it's what Jesus said.'

The good shepherd The second analogy is more familiar. As we've seen
earlier in our journey, the Bible often uses the image of a shepherd and
sheep to communicate God's relationship with his people (Isaiah
40:11, Ezekiel 34:12). In this passage Jesus emphasises two details of
the picture of shepherd and sheep:

The first is the shepherd's *voice*. Jesus' followers can enjoy close
relationship with him (10:14); they will recognise his voice (10:4,5).
He is not an impersonal 'higher being'. He knows your name (10:3);
he cares about you like a shepherd who recognises and loves his sheep.
The second detail is the shepherd's *willingness to sacrifice himself*
(10:11,15). Jesus is clearly foreshadowing what he would later do on
the cross.

Some felt threatened by Jesus' teaching and chose to reject him
(10:20) – and that still happens today. Jesus offers new life: 'I have
come that they may have life, and have it to the full' (10:10).

APPLY   Why do you think some people have so much trouble
believing that Jesus is the only way to God?

PRAY   Spend some time praying for one person you know who's
struggling with the idea that Jesus is the way to God.

55   The vineyard church

Date: *More parables of Jesus*

PRAY   Father, I'm so thankful that you are in charge of this world and my life. I come to you today confident that you know what's best for me.

READ   John 15:1–17

REFLECT

It's important to understand the context in which Jesus introduced this next figure of speech. In chapters 14–17, John records an extended, private teaching session that Jesus had with his disciples the night before he was arrested and then crucified. Our passage today is part of Jesus' last opportunity to communicate the nature of his relationship with his Father and his followers. It was a tough challenge, so he used a familiar image – a vine and its branches.

Let's start by clarifying the basics: Jesus says he's the vine, his followers are the branches and God is the gardener. That would be easy to remember. But think about all the things that such a simple analogy would communicate: The gardener is in charge; the vine holds everything together; the branches can't live apart from the vine. What other lessons do you see?

Jesus goes on to emphasise two specific points about the analogy that he felt were especially important.

Fruit The main job of the branches was to bear fruit: that is, for Jesus' followers to do the things he's been instructing them to do (15:7,8). That's still true today. The most important thing we can do in life is not be successful, or wealthy or recognised. It's to bear 'fruit that will last' (15:16). Is that the goal of your life?

Love Jesus didn't encourage his disciples with some Disney-style platitude: 'Just follow your hearts.' Instead, he commanded them to love one another (15:17). That's tough work, especially since he set the ultimate standard (15:13). True love involves both obedience to God's commands and sacrifice for the good of others. Is that kind of love evident in your life?

APPLY   How could you work more this coming month on Jesus' encouragement to grow fruit and increase love?

PRAY   Jesus, help me have goals in my life that include being fruitful in lasting ways for you, and showing people your love.

DISCUSSION QUESTIONS: MORE PARABLES OF JESUS

After you've completed the five readings in this section, get together with another person or group to talk about the things you've learned. Begin by sharing the insights you gained from your own reflection on the passages. Then use the following questions to help you continue the conversation.

1   Have you ever seen or experienced examples of the 'kingdom of heaven' happening here on earth that remind you of Jesus' story descriptions? What were they like?

2   Jesus taught that his salvation is a free gift to us. Why do you think most religions of the world are based on the idea that we can somehow earn salvation?

3   If salvation is really a gift, is there any need for doing good deeds? Why bother to be 'good' if you can't earn your salvation?

4   Jesus' teaching about judgement was pretty uncompromising. Do you think preaching and teaching about judgement should have greater or lesser emphasis in churches today? Why?

5   Today, some people are offended that Jesus is the only way to God. What do you think? Is it acceptable to express this view in public?

6   In what ways should a Christian bear fruit? Should all believers bear the same kind of fruit? Is there some fruit that all followers of Christ should have?

7   As we seek to imitate the self-giving of Jesus, what are the best examples of sacrificial love that you've seen in your lifetime?

THE MIRACLES OF JESUS

Thomas Jefferson (third president of the US, 1801–1809) was fascinated by Jesus. He believed that the ethical teachings of Jesus were the greatest the world had ever known. As a result, Jefferson put together a book entitled *The Life and Morals of Jesus of Nazareth*. For it, he sifted through every verse in the four Gospels and extracted only those which he thought expressed the pure principles of Jesus. He then arranged the selected verses into chronological order. Over time the volume became known as *The Jefferson Bible* and for many years it was distributed to every new member of the US Congress.

But a review of *The Jefferson Bible* today quickly reveals that something very important is missing: Jefferson removed all references to Jesus' miracles or to his resurrection. Although Thomas Jefferson believed Jesus was a great moral teacher, he simply couldn't accept the supernatural aspects of his life and ministry.

In our next 10 readings, we'll consider the miracles of Jesus. The first set is a collection of five 'supernatural events' – changing water into wine, calming the sea, feeding more than 5,000 people from a few loaves of bread and fish, walking on water, and causing a fig tree to wither.

In fact, *all* of Jesus' miracles could be called supernatural, but this first set highlights his power to overrule the forces of nature. In the second set we'll cover six healing miracles of Jesus. Once we've completed these readings, which cover much of the material Thomas Jefferson removed from his 'Bible', we'll see why the miracles are an indispensable part of the **EssentialJESUS**.

We'll also discover that Jesus performed miracles for a variety of reasons. Of course, at the most basic level, Jesus wanted to meet the needs of the people around him. But, beyond that, Jesus' miracles were *signs* that had two other purposes. As John tells us at the end of his account of Jesus' first miracle – turning water into wine – they *revealed his glory* and they *helped people put their faith in him*. Jesus' miracles were intended to help people believe that he was the Son of God, which is why it's important not to skip over them.

56

New wine

Date:

The miracles of Jesus

PRAY   Father, sometimes my understanding of you seems tired or stale. Please guide me into a fresh, new relationship with you.

READ   John 2:1–11

REFLECT

I once attended a wedding where the caterer's van, loaded with all the food, was stolen before the reception. While the hosts scrambled behind the scenes to solve the problem, the guests waited and waited... and then began discussing how they could help. In the end, the hosts somehow found enough food for everyone and the wedding was a great success.

Perhaps a desire to help was the original motivation behind Mary's comment to her son at this wedding (2:3). But, judging from Jesus' response, it seems she also had something else in mind. She wanted everyone to know the secret she had been pondering all these years: her son was God's promised Messiah, the Saviour of the world (Luke 2:19). It's only natural for a mother to want to show off her son.

But Jesus always resisted the temptation to use his power to show off (John 7:3–9). By saying, 'My time has not yet come,' he makes clear he had a much bigger agenda in mind. Jesus had come to fulfill the mission given to him by his heavenly Father, not his earthly mother.

John adds a comment to make sure his readers get the point (2:11). Jesus performed miracles first of all because they *revealed his glory*. They were evidence of his divine nature. But, second, they *helped people put their faith in him*. Jesus' mission was to help people believe that he was the Son of God.

So what is the significance of his first miracle? Some have said Jesus was blessing the use of wine, or that he was affirming the value of celebration. That may be part of it. But the deeper significance is far more profound. Jesus was signalling that he came to establish a new way for people to have a relationship with God – a way based not on keeping the Law of Moses (the complex list of rules begun with the Ten Commandments), but rather on having faith in him. The good news is that through Jesus we can now have this new relationship with God.

APPLY   What things in your spiritual life are *old* and need to be replaced by something *new* from Jesus?

PRAY   Jesus, show me how I can experience more of the new life you came to give.

57

Fear factor

The miracles of Jesus

PRAY   Lord, I pray that as I come to your Word today, you
would use it to meet the deepest needs in my life.

READ   Mark 4:35–41

REFLECT

The facts of this passage are fairly straightforward: Jesus and his
disciples are in a boat when a storm blows in. Jesus commands the
storm to stop, and it does. This dramatic miracle reveals another
aspect of our supernatural Jesus: *he has power over the forces of nature.*
That's pretty impressive.

But if I had been in that boat with the disciples, I might have felt Jesus'
questions at the end (4:40) were a little unfair. 'You bet we were
afraid. While you were sleeping *we almost got killed*!' Anyone who's ever
been out on a boat in a big storm (or even a rough sea) knows the
feeling of powerlessness and fear that comes from being out of
control.

Fear is something everyone struggles with at some point. Occasionally
we may find ourselves in physical danger. But more often our fears
come from pondering the endless number of worst-case scenarios that
threaten us: failure at work, financial disaster, broken relationships,
being alone, deteriorating health, death.

But that's the point behind Jesus' seemingly unfair questions: things
are never out of control when we are with him. When we belong to
Jesus it doesn't matter what happens, it doesn't matter how bad things
get. Jesus has the power to change not only the wind and the waves,
but also every force at work in our lives.

Of course, it would be nice to think that believing in Jesus would
immediately remove all fear from our lives. But the truth is, like the
disciples in the boat, we are human; we lose control and become
fearful. It happens to me all the time. But that's when we need to force
ourselves back to the message of this miracle: with Jesus we have
nothing to fear. Faith doesn't mean that we'll never face danger, or
even that bad things will never happen to us. Instead, faith means
believing that Jesus is all-powerful and knowing that we belong to
him.

APPLY   What are your biggest fears? Look at each one in turn.
What are the root causes of those fears?

PRAY   Honestly talk to Jesus about the things that you fear. Ask
him to give you a surer faith in his control of your life.

58   Miracle meal

Date: *The miracles of Jesus*

PRAY   Sometimes I feel I don't have the resources to solve the biggest problems in my life. Please open my eyes, Lord, to your perspective on the challenges I face.

READ   Matthew 14:13–21

REFLECT

It must have been difficult at times to be a disciple of Jesus; he was constantly testing them. Sometimes he led them into tough situations. At other times he asked them tough questions. But, all the time, you get the sense that Jesus was trying to build their trust in him. He still does that with us today.

That's what's going on in this familiar miracle. Jesus already knows he can feed the 5,000 men plus twice as many women and children (14:21). But, before he does, he challenges the disciples to solve the problem. What's your first instinct when you face a big problem? Do you come up with a plan? Do you complain? Do you go into high-energy mode? Do you get paralysed with worry?

Here, the disciples' first instinct was to look at their own resources (14:17), and their conclusion was they didn't have enough to solve the problem. Not even close. But what Jesus was probing was whether or not his disciples would look to him first to solve the problem. Note that he says, 'Bring them here to me' (14:18). In other words, 'Remember who I am; look to me first in everything that happens.' It was the very same principle he taught in the Sermon on the Mount (Matthew 6:33).

I've always been curious about how Jesus did this miracle; at the critical point, the text simply says, 'They all ate and were satisfied' (14:20). I once saw a play about Jesus that included this miracle. In it, the empty-handed disciples huddled with Jesus in a rugby scrum – and then suddenly burst out with armloads of Italian bread. I don't know how they did that either!

We don't know how or when Jesus will intervene in our lives. All we need to know is that he can, and he has resources far greater than we can ever imagine (Psalm 50:10). And that was the point of this miraculous picnic.

APPLY   What is the single biggest problem you face now? What would it mean for you to 'look to Jesus' for a solution?

PRAY   Lord Jesus, life is filled with problems. I'm thankful that you know my needs and want me to come to you.

59

Seeing and believing

Date:

The miracles of Jesus

PRAY   Heavenly Father, as I read today, strengthen any areas
where my faith is weak.

READ   Matthew 14:22–33

REFLECT

I saw a television interview with an actor from the movie *The Da Vinci
Code*. In response to criticism that the movie made untrue statements
about Jesus, the actor said, 'Well, I've always felt the Bible should
include a disclaimer. A man walking on water... ? Come on!'

But just because we haven't seen something doesn't mean it can't be
true. Peter had never seen a man walking on water either; it might
have been a mirage or a ghost or something worse. Still, he stepped
out of the boat. That's the essence of faith: the willingness to move
forward, trusting God even when the way is unclear.

I wonder what Peter felt in that moment when he realised he was
sinking into the raging waters? Embarrassment? Panic? Fear?
Probably all of that. Now try to imagine Peter's emotions when he felt
the strong grip of Jesus on his arm. That was the moment he was sure
it was no ghost. Once Peter was safely back in the boat, there was no
need to quibble about whether a man could walk on water.

I remember facing a situation that scared the daylights out of me. I
was inadvertently drawn into a financial scam that threatened to wipe
me out. During those days, I typed the words that Jesus said to the
disciples on a piece of paper and taped it to my work station.
Whenever I felt fearful, I'd look at the words and say them aloud:
'Take courage! It is I. Don't be afraid' (14:27). I learned the lesson
Peter learned from the middle of the lake: calling out to Jesus is the
best way to overcome fear.

So how might I respond to that actor who wouldn't believe that Jesus
walked on water? All I can say is this: I know Jesus has saved me. I've
experienced his ability to take away my fear. So it doesn't seem so
unbelievable that he could also walk on water. And I don't need to see
it to believe it.

APPLY   In what area of your life do you need to trust Jesus and
move forward in faith, even though the way seems
unclear? How could you do so?

PRAY   Spend a few minutes praying about any area where you
sense a need to step out in faith.

60

Serious fruit

Date:

The miracles of Jesus

PRAY   Father, build my faith as I read your Word and pray
today.

READ   Matthew 21:18–22

REFLECT

It would be much easier for us to focus our attention here on Jesus'
encouraging comments about 'mountain-moving faith' rather than on
how he miraculously withered the poor fig tree. But the two actions
were linked and were intended to teach the disciples – and us – some
important truths.

Some might explain Jesus' outburst as a reaction to pressure. Even
when they're stressed out, Christian leaders need to remember the
feelings of others; they also need the understanding and forgiveness of
those around them. It's hard to be perfect when you are in the public
eye all the time.

But was this what was going on here? I believe the point of Jesus' sharp
words and miraculous withering of the fig tree was not about relieving
stress but about bearing fruit. Some commentators see the fig tree as a
symbol of Israel's religion at the time; it looked good but ultimately
was not satisfying the people's spiritual hunger. But it also seems to be
a statement by Jesus on the urgency of his mission. He wanted his
followers to know that bearing fruit is serious business and there is no
time to waste.

Producing fruit involves at least two things: *faith* and *prayer*. This is
something far different from what some preachers call 'naming and
claiming'. It is *faith built on a deep relationship with our heavenly Father*
and *prayer that changes us so that we can submit to his will* – which may
be radically different from our original request.

But when we have waited before the Lord and honestly perceived his
purposes, we can approach our 'mountains' with confidence that he
will move them. Jesus reminds us that the size of the mountain is not a
problem for God. Our challenge is to develop the kind of prayer life
that is built on an unwavering trust that God will accomplish his
purposes, his way. As we do that, we can expect him to do incredible
things in our lives.

APPLY   In what area of your life do you most need to experience
'mountain-moving faith'? What step could you take in
that direction today?

PRAY   Ask Jesus to give you a sense of urgency about growing
his fruit in your life.

DISCUSSION QUESTIONS: THE MIRACLES OF JESUS

After you've completed the five readings in this section, get together with another person or group to talk about the things you've learned. Begin by sharing the insights you gained from your own reflection on the passages. Then use the following questions to help you continue the conversation.

1   Reflect on some of the supernatural things you've read about in the actions of Jesus. How would you define a miracle? Do you think miracles still happen today? Have you ever experienced one? Share your experiences.

2   Why do people try to explain away the miracles of Jesus recorded in the Bible with explanations borrowed from science?

3   Can you think of a time in your life when you were overwhelmed by fear? What happened and what helped you cope? Has faith in Jesus ever helped you at such times? How?

4   Has Jesus ever miraculously provided for you? What happened?

5   Is there anything you've so far encountered in these readings about the life and ministry of Jesus that seems unbelievable to you? If so, what is it and why?

6   How would you articulate 'the case for Christ'? If you had to present belief in him in a court of law, what would be the most convincing evidence that he was the Son of God?

MORE MIRACLES OF JESUS

I don't blame people today for being sceptical about healing. I once watched a television documentary on a well-known faith healer. The cameras rolled as people from the audience were helped onto the stage. After the faith healer put his hands on them and dramatically prayed, people threw away crutches, got up out of wheelchairs or reported instant recovery from disease... all to great applause. But when the documentary-makers followed up months later, they had trouble finding anyone who was still 'healed'.

Even so, most people still believe genuine healing is possible. Why? First, because suffering and sickness are so awful; in our desperation we become open to possibilities we would not be willing to consider when everything is just fine. And second, because there are many documented examples of real healing throughout history. Not only that, medical professionals today regularly report unexplained recoveries. And just about everyone knows somebody who has experienced a miraculous healing. We may not understand or agree on the reasons why, but we have to admit one thing: healing happens.

The challenge for us in the next five readings is to examine the healing miracles of Jesus with an open mind. We'll read how Jesus enabled a blind man to see, caused a paralysed man to walk, restored a demon-possessed man, cured a woman with an incurable bleeding problem and brought two dead people back to life. These accounts are some of the most exciting and inspiring parts of Jesus' entire ministry.

They also give us a deeper understanding of the **EssentialJESUS**. The most basic thing we learn is that Jesus had *compassion* for people; he wasn't too busy or important to help people overcome their problems. Next, the healing miracles of Jesus demonstrate his *power* and *authority*, not just over sickness, but also over sin. Finally, the healings provide us with more evidence of his *divinity*. Jesus was who he said he was, the Son of God.

That's a lot to absorb. So let's read through the healings one by one. As you do, try to imagine that you are there. Perhaps you could be the person receiving the healing, or one of the disciples, or even a person in the crowd. What would you have felt and said and done? Try to step into the story so you can experience the healing ministry of Jesus for yourself.

61

'Lord, I believe'

Date: *More miracles of Jesus*

PRAY   Father, 'open my eyes that I may see wonderful things in your law' today (Psalm 119:18).

READ   John 9

REFLECT

Even a junior reporter could get the facts of this story straight: JERUSALEM – *An itinerant preacher from Galilee named Jesus sparked controversy earlier today. According to eyewitnesses, Jesus and his entourage met a man who was blind from birth as they walked on the main road near Jerusalem. After a brief dialogue, Jesus put mud on the man's eyes, told him to wash in a local pond and the man's eyesight was restored. Religious leaders have challenged the validity of the 'healing' and have launched their own investigation.*

Why is it so difficult for some to accept the fact that Jesus heals people? The Pharisees were more concerned about defending a set of picky religious rules than they were about experiencing God. When told about the healing, they condemned it on a technicality (9:16). If we ever let good things like our church traditions or our theological positions get in the way of our passion for meeting God, then something is off track.

The blind man was the only one who saw the light (9:5)! Instead of questioning or challenging Jesus, he simply *obeyed* (9:7). Next, he honestly *shared his experience* with others (9:11,25), even defending it in spite of the pressure tactics used against him (9:24–34). Finally, after taking time to think it through, he *put his faith in Jesus* (9:38). Perhaps the strongest proof of the validity of this miracle was the fact that the blind man never backed down. He could easily have changed his story, or at least shaped it just a little, to satisfy the Pharisees and avoid 'excommunication'. But he didn't... he couldn't... because he could see!

The Pharisees rejected the healing because Jesus didn't fit into their religious system. Their attitude was, 'How dare you lecture us!' The disciples might have missed it; their interest seemed more theological than personal: 'Who sinned... that he was born blind?' But the blind man was healed because he was open-minded about what Jesus could do. That's the first step to true faith: 'Lord, I believe.'

APPLY   Why do some people keep their minds closed about Jesus today?

PRAY   Lord, give me the courage to be a bolder witness for you, like the man who was born blind.

62

Band of brothers

Date: *More miracles of Jesus*

PRAY   Spend a few minutes talking to God about any
              circumstances in your life that paralyse you – physically,
              emotionally or spiritually…

READ   Luke 5:17–26

REFLECT

You have to feel sorry for the poor Pharisees and the teachers of the
Law. They were always on the defensive. Jesus was always right and in
control of the circumstances, and it infuriated them. I can picture
these pompous religious leaders, sitting there in the front row, arms
folded, scowling as Jesus healed people. They were angry. When we
find ourselves angry with God over the circumstances in our lives, we
should take time to reflect on the underlying source of our anger.
There may be an inconvenient truth we've been avoiding.

On the other hand, you have to feel love for the band of brothers who
carried their friend to Jesus. I can imagine the hard work it took to lug
a paralysed man across town. He was heavy; it took four men to lift
him. And it would perhaps have been embarrassing. But they persisted
for at least two reasons:

They loved their friend and showed it by sacrificial work. *They believed
Jesus could make a difference.* It was a simple strategy, but it still works
today: bring your friends to Jesus.

Imagine the commotion and drama as the man on the stretcher was
lowered through the roof; it took guts and creativity to try a stunt like
that. It also took faith, as Jesus pointed out (5:20). It's significant that
Jesus healed the man because of *'their* faith'. Sometimes God
intervenes in the lives of people based on the faith of those around
them. It's a reality that should energise our prayer and service for
others.

Unfortunately the grumpy old Pharisees rejected Jesus in spite of the
evidence that was clear to everyone else: the paralysed man walked out
of the meeting praising God (5:25). They knew exactly what the
deeper issue was: if they admitted Jesus had authority to forgive sins,
they were admitting that he was God (5:21), and that was the one
thing they weren't willing to do.

APPLY   How could you take a step of faith in Jesus' power on
              behalf of someone close to you?

PRAY   Spend a few moments asking Jesus to restore those areas
              of your life that need spiritual or physical healing. End
              with a time of praise.

63

Scary story?

More miracles of Jesus

PRAY   Father, please give me a deeper sense of your power over
sin and love for me as I spend time reading your Word
today.

READ   Mark 5:1–20

REFLECT

The reality of demon possession is difficult for modern minds to
accept. It has become a popular plot line for horror films. It's also a
comic device: the cartoon image of a red-tailed 'alter ego' sitting on
someone's shoulder whispering devious thoughts of revenge always
gets a laugh. But actual demon possession? That doesn't happen
today, right?

Yet, from beginning to end, the Bible teaches that the devil is real, and
that he's hell-bent on opposing God and destroying people.

We see a vivid example of that in our passage today. The devil had
been at work in this poor man's life for a long time, torturing his mind
and body, and in the process alienating the man from himself and
from society. But Jesus stepped in:

Jesus took control of the situation and of the demons themselves (5:6–
8). Clearly, Jesus was the higher power.

Jesus dealt with the demons once and for all (5:11–13), something the
townspeople had never been able to do (5:4).

Jesus restored the man and gave him a renewed purpose in life (5:18–
20). Often those with the darkest pasts become the most effective
witnesses for God.

But this passage also contains two great ironies:

The demons knew who Jesus really was. They almost sound like
theologians: 'What do you want with me, Jesus, Son of the Most High
God?' (5:7).

The townspeople were afraid instead of rejoicing. They pleaded with Jesus
to leave. Maybe they thought Jesus was out to ruin their economy;
2,000 pigs represented a lot of money. Or maybe they were nervous
he'd come after the skeletons in *their* closets next. Whatever the
reason, they pushed Jesus out of their lives.

APPLY   Is there a skeleton lurking in the closet of your heart?
What will it take for you to bring this issue 'into the
light', to Jesus?

PRAY   Pray about any unresolved issues in your past that need
healing.

64

At his feet

More miracles of Jesus

PRAY Lord, my life is so complicated and stressful; sometimes I feel like I've run out of answers. Right now I humbly bow before you and wait for your peace and help.

READ Mark 5:21–43

REFLECT

Politicians work hard to get 'Big Mo' on their side; in the US it's the insider's term for 'momentum' and it's what wins elections. Jesus was no politician but, at this point in his ministry, Big Mo was definitely working for him. His authoritative teaching and dramatic miracles were causing big crowds to follow him everywhere he went (5:21,24). Our passage today weaves together the accounts of two miracles that occurred during this exciting and chaotic time in Jesus' ministry.

A very private healing An unnamed woman in the crowd had suffered from uncontrollable bleeding for 12 years (5:25). Long-term physical problems often lead to emotional and spiritual depression as well. Difficult though it may be, God sometimes allows us to experience a 'dark night of the soul' in order to help us see our need for him, as he did for this woman. Her friends may have criticised her desperate scheme (5:28). But Jesus said, 'Your faith has healed you' (5:34). Sometimes faith requires us to take desperate measures.

A very public healing The daughter of a well-known synagogue ruler named Jairus – a man who would have been aligned with groups opposing Jesus – had fallen sick. Once again we see God using a health emergency to produce true faith. As Dr C Everett Koop, a paediatric surgeon and former Surgeon General of the US, once said, 'There are no atheists at the bedside of a dying child.' His colleagues may have criticised Jairus for being a turncoat. But Jesus said, 'Don't be afraid; just believe' (5:36). Sometimes faith requires us to ignore what others think.

A common element in both of these healings is the way the unnamed woman and Jairus approached Jesus. They 'fell at his feet' (5:22,33). The surest way to experience Jesus' healing power is to reach out humbly to him and then wait for him to respond in his way.

APPLY Have you ever needed to take desperate measures or ignore what others think to exercise faith? What happened?

PRAY Bring to God in prayer the area of your life where you feel the greatest sense of desperation…

65

Resurrection power

Date: *More miracles of Jesus*

PRAY   Dear Lord, please help me to understand what it means to experience 'the power of his resurrection' (Philippians 3:10) today.

READ   John 11:1–45

REFLECT

For Jesus, this miracle was a very personal demonstration of his power. Lazarus, Martha and Mary were his close friends. He had eaten with them (Luke 10:38–42), cried with them (11:35) and come to love them deeply (11:3). His relationship with them reminds us of a vital truth about Jesus; in addition to being the Son of God, he was also a real man. He understands what it's like to be human. He's been where we are (Hebrews 4:15).

For the religious leaders, this miracle was the last straw. Jesus was enjoying growing popularity and it frustrated his opponents no end. 'Eventually, though, public attention will shift,' they must have thought, 'and we'll be back in the headlines.' But when Jesus brought Lazarus back to life, the chief priests and Pharisees went over to the dark side for good (11:49–53). There was no way to stop someone with the power over life and death.

But that's exactly what Jesus claimed; he was the resurrection and the life (11:25,26). Instead of seeing this as a threat, his followers then and now understand what a wonderful promise it is: believing in Jesus is the way to eternal life (John 14:6). The Bible teaches that the resurrection of Jesus was the ultimate validation of his divine nature and mission (1 Corinthians 15). This miraculous raising of Lazarus as well as the raising of Jairus' daughter were early signs of the greatest resurrection that was soon to come, when God raised his own Son, Jesus Christ, from the dead.

There's an interesting detail buried in this dramatic miracle. Earlier, Martha had been the fussy complainer, too distracted to be with Jesus (Luke 10:38–42). Now she's the one with time to talk with Jesus about the deepest truths concerning his resurrection (11:24). Just because we've had weak moments, or times of confusion about Jesus, doesn't mean we can't keep growing in our faith. Thank God.

APPLY   A popular country song says, 'Everybody wants to go to heaven, but nobody wants to die.' How do you feel about that?

PRAY   Are you able to use Martha's words as your prayer? 'Yes, Lord … I believe that you are the Christ, the Son of God, who has come into the world.'

DISCUSSION QUESTIONS: MORE MIRACLES OF JESUS

After you've completed the five readings in this section, get together with another person or group to talk about the things you've learned. Begin by sharing the insights you gained from your own reflection on the passages. Then use the following questions to help you continue the conversation.

1   Why do you think some people are sceptical about the healing power of Jesus? What's your opinion about the possibility of healing today?

2   Have you or someone close to you ever experienced what you would consider a miraculous healing? What happened?

3   Have you prayed and not been healed? How has that affected your faith in Jesus?

4   What have you learned about Jesus in looking at the way he handled demon possession? Do you think it's okay to watch movies or television programmes about demon possession? Why?

5   Like the friends brought the paralysed man, how could you bring more of your friends to Jesus? Is that your responsibility?

6   Why is it so significant that Jesus raised Jairus' daughter and Lazarus from the dead? What did that signal to the religious leaders of that time? What does it signal to you?

THE PRAYERS OF JESUS

What's the first thing that comes to your mind when you think about the prayers of Jesus? Exactly — the Lord's Prayer! 'Our Father who art in heaven, hallowed be thy name... ' It's the most repeated prayer in all of human history, with the possible exception of, 'Lord, save me!'

Prayer is one of those things that almost everyone has tried, but almost no one fully understands. That's why our next five readings will be so helpful; they give us a picture of the greatest 'pray-er' the world has ever known. The disciples recognised that there was something special about the way Jesus prayed. After observing him, one of the disciples spoke up for people throughout the ages when he said, 'Lord, teach us to pray... ' (Luke 11:1). If you want to learn how to pray, watch someone who knows how to do it. And you'll find no better teacher than Jesus.

What we learn when we examine the prayers of Jesus is that he prayed in all kinds of situations and in all kinds of ways. Of course, he prayed the famous model prayer we call the Lord's Prayer, which forms a memorable outline for anyone who wants good topics for prayer (Luke 11:1–13). He prayed spontaneous prayers when good things happened in his ministry (Luke 10:1–24). He prayed long formal prayers when he had far-reaching issues on his mind (John 17). And he prayed short intense prayers when he was under great pressure (Mark 14:32–42).

But as we examine these wonderful prayers, we may want to ask ourselves an important question: why did Jesus pray? After all, he was the Son of God; he had all the power of heaven at his disposal and could do anything he wanted. The answer to that question takes us to the heart of what prayer is all about. Jesus prayed because his relationship with his heavenly Father was the most important thing to him. That's why he spent so much time talking to God, listening to God and simply spending time in God's presence.

Perhaps the greatest lesson we can learn is that Jesus didn't pray just at set times or on special occasions; he prayed whenever he could (Mark 1:29–39). There's a sense in which Jesus was constantly praying; his mind and heart were always focused on his heavenly Father – and that's the essence of prayer. As you're about to discover, prayer was essential for Jesus. And, if that's so, it's even more essential for us.

66   How did Jesus pray?

Date: *The prayers of Jesus*

PRAY   Father, in spite of all the distractions, my heart's desire is
             to deepen my relationship with you.

READ   Mark 1:29–39

REFLECT

Have you ever observed someone who is praying, silently and
intensely, particularly someone who's known God for a while? You
can't hear anything, but you can feel that something important is
happening. That's the opportunity we have in this passage; we're
watching the world's greatest 'prayer warrior' in action and in so doing
we gain unique insights into the prayer life of Jesus.

He prayed whatever. Jesus must have been exhausted (1:32–34) and
out of his normal routine; he was a guest in someone else's home
(1:29–31). Those are two things that often derail my prayer life.

He prayed early. Jesus got up early to pray, 'while it was still dark'.
Prayer was the first thing on his mind for the day. What do you first
think about when you get out of bed?

He prayed without distraction. Jesus went to a 'solitary place' to pray.
Effective prayer often means leaving behind the distractions of life –
though Jesus is always ready to answer our prayer from the midst of
frantic activity too! Jesus prayed in spite of the well-meaning pressure
from his disciples (1:37). We'll always feel the pressure to get busy, but
without prayer it's difficult to make a difference for God.

As we read the Gospels we find other references to Jesus' pattern of
prayer (Luke 6:12; Matthew 14:23; 26:36). If you sometimes feel
guilty because you can't pray for long, try praying more often
throughout the day. You may find yourself feeling less guilty and more
excited about your dialogue with God. And that's what prayer is all
about. Because Jesus' mind and heart were always focused on doing
his Father's will, he was always praying – sometimes privately,
sometimes formally and sometimes in the middle of the action. Too
often we have to make time for prayer in the midst of our busy lives.
For Jesus, interacting with his heavenly Father was the central task of
his entire life. He made time for everything else.

APPLY   How could you make prayer less of an activity and more
             of a lifestyle?

PRAY   Experiment with a different approach to talking to Jesus
             today. For example, even if you are alone, pray aloud. Or
             try a different posture, or go outside and look at the sky
             as you pray, or take a 'prayer walk', or...

67

The joy of prayer

Date:

The prayers of Jesus

PRAY   Begin with a time of praise: 'Praise the LORD, O my soul; all my inmost being, praise his holy name' (Psalm 103:1).

READ   Luke 10:1–24

REFLECT

This was a moment to savour. The 72 missionaries had returned with reports of effective outreach (10:17). You can imagine Jesus giving 'high fives' to each one as they went around the circle sharing their experiences. But, in the middle of this victory celebration, Jesus took time for an impromptu prayer meeting (10:21). We can take two important pointers from this prayer:

Emphasis on joy The missionaries were feeling the joy of success; they had obeyed Jesus and seen results. That principle still works today. But Jesus' joy was more profound because he saw the deeper reality of what was happening. Verse 21 says he was 'full of joy through the Holy Spirit'. Satan, the real enemy, was being defeated (10:18) and God's self-revelation was becoming more clear and understandable – even to the most unlikely persons (10:21). Too often, prayer can become a solemn recitation of problems and worries. But when we really understand what God is doing in the world, it makes us want to shout for joy.

Confidence in God's plan 'Yes, Father, for this was your good pleasure' (10:21). Some people think of prayer as a kind of hopeless, wishful thinking: 'Oh well, all I can do now is pray. Maybe I'll get lucky.' But when we really understand that God is in control of everything, we can be bold. Confidence in God's power and will is another vital part of prayer.

In spite of this inspiring prayer, Jesus knew his followers would eventually face difficulties, so he gave them two important reminders:

Live with the kingdom in mind. No matter what happens, whether we experience success or failure, living with the *kingdom* end in mind (10:20) puts everything else into proper perspective.

Live with the big picture in mind. God has been at work for a long time (10:23,24) drawing people to himself, and he will continue to do so. Our responsibility is not to achieve success, but to remain faithful to God – another reason we need to pray.

APPLY   What things about Jesus make you feel the most joyful?

PRAY   Praise Jesus with these words: 'I will shout for joy and sing your praises, for you have ransomed me' (Psalm 71:23, NLT).

68   The school of prayer

Date: *The prayers of Jesus*

PRAY   Close your eyes and concentrate on the fact that God is really with you in the room. How do you feel? What are you thinking? Now, what would you like to say to him?

READ   Luke 11:1–13

REFLECT

If someone asked you to help them develop a deeper prayer life, how would you respond? By explaining your prayer habits? By sharing a book on the subject? By suggesting a helpful tape or seminar? Jesus begins his response by simply praying. If you want to get better at praying, he seems to say, don't spend too much time studying it. Just pray.

The Lord's Prayer (see also Matthew 6:9–15) is undoubtedly the most famous and most repeated prayer in history. Over the centuries, many of the Church's best minds have analysed this prayer. But for our purposes we note that effective prayer involves two perspectives, which need to be in balance:

Beyond us In prayer we look beyond ourselves to God, his nature, his holiness, his kingdom and his will (11:2).

Close to us Yet we should not hesitate to focus on our day-to-day needs – food, forgiveness and strength to avoid temptation (11:3,4).

Jesus then encourages *boldness* (11:5–10). Does that mean we can ask for new cars, big bank accounts and dream houses? Not exactly. Jesus' story, as well as other passages in the Bible (Matthew 6:8; 26:42; Philippians 4:19), reminds us to focus on our genuine needs, not our selfish wants.

Jesus also reflects on prayer from God's perspective and the analogy he uses is a loving father caring for a needy child (11:11–13). God loves us and he knows what is truly best. Our mistake is we want to tell him what 'good gift' he must give us. Sometimes we need to let go of what we think is the best solution to our problems and pray for an acceptance of his will, whatever that may be. Jesus assures us that a heart attitude of faith in our loving heavenly Father, combined with a bold persistence in prayer, will get incredible results (Matthew 17:20,21).

APPLY   What is one situation in your life that needs bold, persistent prayer to Jesus? Is it a need or a want?

PRAY   Spend time talking to Jesus about the biggest current problem in your life.

69

Date: *The prayers of Jesus*

PRAY   Ask God for both a greater knowledge and a deeper experience of him as you spend time in his Word.

READ   John 17

REFLECT

Wouldn't you like to know if and what famous people prayed before their defining moments in history? Did Winston Churchill pray as he waited for D-day? How did Mother Teresa pray as she began her life's work among the deprived of Calcutta? And what was the prayer of William Wilberforce as he waited for his bill for the abolition of slavery to be voted on? In this passage, we read what Jesus prayed just before the most significant event of his life: death on the cross.

Jesus had just given his confused and anxious disciples their final instructions (John 13–16), concluding with this, often referred to as the 'high priestly prayer', in which he prayed for his disciples and all believers.

Jesus begins by praying for himself (17:1–5). He recognises that 'the time has come' for him to complete his God-given mission. For Jesus, that meant re-establishing a way for humankind to know God and have eternal life.

Jesus then prays for his disciples (17:6–19), asking for three things:

Protection (17:11,15) Anyone who attempts to follow Jesus will face attacks from the devil.

Joy (17:13) He's not talking about a happy feeling. He's talking about the deep satisfaction that comes from being one with Jesus and part of what he's doing in the world, which gives us significance and reason to rejoice.

Holiness (17:17) He prays that his followers be sanctified – set apart or made holy – by the Word of God, which is why Bible reading and prayer make such a powerful combination.

Jesus also prays for everyone who would believe in him as a result of the disciples' message (17:20–26) – and that includes you and me. His main request is for unity. Even though the institutional Church has become divided and weakened over the centuries, the universal Church is still one body.

APPLY   How could you promote greater unity among the followers of Jesus you know?

PRAY   Spend some time talking to God about any defining moment that looms on the horizon of your life.

70   Pray hard

Date: *The prayers of Jesus*

PRAY   Father, I'm so grateful that you are willing to accept me as your child. How wonderful to know that the all-powerful Creator of the Universe knows and cares about me.

READ   Mark 14:32–42

REFLECT

Persecuted Christians around the world live in fear of a knock on the door in the middle of the night. We've all faced anxious moments when we know something awful is about to happen, but all we can do is wait. Here Jesus feels 'deeply distressed and troubled ... overwhelmed with sorrow to the point of death' (14:33,34) as he waits for his accusers to show up and arrest him. I've always felt this is the most intense prayer Jesus ever prayed.

So how did Jesus pray when he was under such pressure? He starts by simply calling out to his Father (14:36). The word 'Abba' literally means 'Dad'.

When our grandson Noah wakes up in the middle of the night, he calls out in his dark room. Even though he's scared, he knows his parents are nearby. That's how Jesus starts this prayer.

Next, Jesus affirms what he knows to be true: all things are possible for God. It brings assurance to remember that we pray to a God who is all-powerful. Jesus then makes his request: 'Take this cup from me'(14:36); in other words, 'If there's another way to accomplish your plan of salvation without sacrificing me, please do it!' There's nothing wrong with being honest with God in prayer. Jesus concludes by accepting God's will, whatever that may be.

The intensity of Jesus' prayer contrasts with the lethargy of the disciples' prayer (14:37–42). I wonder if Jesus was tempted to give Peter a kick. It's interesting that Jesus rebuked Peter with his old name, Simon; the leading disciple had gone back to his old habits. But, before we condemn the sleepy prayer habits of the disciples, we should admit there are times when our prayers are less than focused. There's a T-shirt I like, showing a man wearing a pair of jeans with holes in both knees. Underneath it simply says, 'Pray hard'. That's exactly what Jesus did at Gethsemane.

APPLY   Can you think of a time when you were under intense pressure? What happened to your relationship with Jesus during that time?

PRAY   Dear Father, I face situations that overwhelm me at times. But, no matter what happens my heart cry is this: not what I will, but what you will.

DISCUSSION QUESTIONS: THE PRAYERS OF JESUS

After you've completed the five readings in this section, get together with another person or group to talk about the things you've learned. Begin by sharing the insights you gained from your own reflection on the passages. Then use the following questions to help you continue the conversation.

1   How did you first learn about prayer? Over the years, have you known any 'prayer warriors' and what have they taught you?

2   What have you learned from the example of Jesus and his prayers?

3   When do you feel that your prayers are the most meaningful and effective? When, if at all, do you experience prayer that makes you feel close to Jesus?

4   Think about the prayer that Jesus 'modelled' for his followers (Luke 11:1–13)? What are the most challenging or meaningful parts for you?

5   Have you ever prayed for Jesus' help at a time when you were under great pressure? What happened? Did that experience change your view of prayer? Of Jesus?

6   What are the biggest obstacles to praying you face? How can you overcome these?

7   How could you develop a 'prayer lifestyle'? What are some new and creative ways you could make prayer a more significant part of your daily life?

THE HARD SAYINGS OF JESUS

In 1742 Charles Wesley wrote the words to the hymn 'Gentle Jesus, Meek and Mild'. It thoughtfully expressed Wesley's desire to simply and completely follow Jesus. But, over the years, I've heard people quote the title of that hymn as a way of expressing a rather simplistic view of Jesus: that he was some kind of sissy who walked around making fluffy moral statements to be memorised in Sunday School or printed on fridge magnets. Gentle Jesus, meek and mild... isn't that nice?

I hate to burst anyone's bubble, but I'm not at all sure that's what Charles Wesley had in mind, and it's certainly not representative of the things Jesus said in his teaching ministry. Certainly, Jesus said some wonderful and encouraging things, as we've been exploring in our journey through the Bible. But, as we're about to discover in our next five readings, Jesus also made many statements that were very difficult to understand. In fact, at one point in his ministry, people were so turned off by his teaching that they said, 'This is a hard saying; who can listen to it?' (John 6:60, RSV) and they deserted him in droves.

Sometimes Jesus said things that were obscure; they were difficult to understand. Other times he said things that were challenging and difficult to obey. We'll be covering some from both categories:

– Whoever eats my flesh and drinks my blood has eternal life.

– Whoever blasphemes against the Holy Spirit will never be forgiven; he is guilty of an eternal sin.

– You may ask me for anything in my name, and I will do it.

– This is how my heavenly Father will treat each of you unless you forgive your brother from your heart.

– If anyone would come after me, he must deny himself and take up his cross and follow me.

If you are intrigued by this line of study, I would suggest that you get a copy of *Hard Sayings of Jesus* by FF Bruce (IVP) which covers 70 of the most challenging statements that Jesus ever made. But for now, five will do, so let's get going.

71

Soul food

The hard sayings of Jesus

PRAY   'My soul will be satisfied as with the richest of foods; with singing lips my mouth will praise you' (Psalm 63:5)...

READ   John 6:25–71

REFLECT

Whoever eats my flesh and drinks my blood has eternal life... (6:54). What a strange comment! It sounds like Jesus has some odd ideas... is this cannibalism? No wonder the disciples were confused and offended (6:60,61); their hero seems to have lost his marbles. 'Couldn't you just re-phrase that a little?' And no wonder the religious leaders are outraged; in addition to the disgusting image of eating human flesh, the Law of Moses contained specific regulations about not consuming blood or even meat with blood in it (Leviticus 17:13,14).

In fact, this is one of the most important statements Jesus ever made. To understand it fully we must step back and look at the context. Jesus has just finished miraculously feeding thousands of people (John 6:1–15). Unfortunately, no one seems to understand the miracle (6:26). Most thought Jesus just liked giving away free food. Pretty cool. But Jesus fed the people to demonstrate that he was the source of eternal life (6:27). From this point on in the dialogue, though, Jesus and his listeners are on two separate tracks: *they* are thinking of worldly realities (food) while *he* is thinking of spiritual realities (eternal life).

And that's the clue we need to understand to what Jesus meant by his perplexing statement. He's not talking about physically eating his flesh and drinking his blood. Rather, he's talking about the spiritual union that he has with his followers. Those who truly put their faith and trust in Jesus are united with God (6:57) and receive eternal life (6:40).

Unfortunately, the more he explains, the more divergent the separate tracks become. His listeners are looking backwards to manna in the desert. Jesus is looking forward to what he would do on the cross.

In our time, we have an opportunity to ponder this spiritual truth whenever we take communion. The bread and wine are reminders of Jesus' sacrifice for us and are 'to be for your people the body and blood of your Son, the holy food of new and unending life in him' (*The Book of Common Prayer, Episcopal Church, US*).

APPLY   Do you ever feel united with Jesus? When? What thoughts go through your mind as you prepare to take the bread and wine of communion?

PRAY   Lord, please help me to draw closer to you. Open my eyes to the spiritual realities of the world I live in.

72

A house divided

Date: *The hard sayings of Jesus*

PRAY   Lord, please give me a better understanding of who you
              are as I read today.

READ   Mark 3:20–35

REFLECT

*But whoever blasphemes against the Holy Spirit will never be forgiven; he is
guilty of an eternal sin* (3:29). When I was growing up, a common
Sunday School question was, 'How can I know if I've committed "the
unforgivable sin" or not?' We were afraid the Bible referred to some
mysterious, unnamed offence. And worse, we worried that if we
unwittingly committed it, we were doomed – with no chance of
getting to heaven.

A careful examination of our passage today shows that Jesus didn't
intend to scare children. Rather, his comment was a sharp rebuke to
the religious leaders who were accusing him of being demon-
possessed (3:30). The leaders had become frustrated with Jesus; he
had been teaching, healing and attracting big crowds (3:20). The
Pharisees got so jealous they were willing to take extreme measures to
protect their turf (Mark 3:6).

That's why they accused Jesus of being demon-possessed (3:22); they
wanted to discredit him in the eyes of the public. In response Jesus
makes two points:

A house divided doesn't stand. The parable Jesus tells easily repels the
false accusation (3:23–27). Satan wouldn't oppose himself. Therefore
Jesus' miracles couldn't be the result of demon-possession.
Interestingly, in 1858 Abraham Lincoln gave a famous speech entitled
A House Divided, referring to this passage, to demonstrate the danger
of dividing the United States into slave and free states.

Unwillingness to repent prevents forgiveness. By equating the work of the
Holy Spirit with demon possession, says Jesus, the religious leaders
were moving 180 degrees away from God. As long as they persisted in
that direction, they could not be forgiven. The truth is, the
'unforgivable sin' is not some secret deed you can unwittingly
commit; Jesus made it clear that he loved to forgive sinners (Luke
15:11–32). Rather, it is an ongoing refusal to accept what Jesus freely
offers that prevents us from being forgiven.

APPLY   Over the past 30 days, have you been moving closer to or
              further away from Jesus?

PRAY   Spend a few minutes confessing your sins to God. Then
              thank him for the forgiveness, love and acceptance he
              offers through a relationship with his Son.

73

Prayer guarantee

The hard sayings of Jesus

PRAY Praise be to God, who has not rejected my prayer or withheld his love from me! (Psalm 66:20).

READ John 14:1–14

REFLECT

You may ask me for anything in my name, and I will do it. Over the years I've heard two reactions to the puzzling statement Jesus made about prayer in this passage (14:14).

'Name it and claim it!' According to this view, we should pray for very specific things, like a new car, a big house or a fat bank account. Isn't that what Jesus said? A friend of mine once commented how odd it was that churches who preached this prosperity gospel often have car parks full of the most dilapidated bangers!

'It ain't necessarily so!' According to this view, we shouldn't pray for specific things. Often, people who feel this way claim they've 'tried prayer' in the past, but it 'didn't work'.

The problem with both views is they focus exclusively on earthly things, and that's misunderstanding what Jesus meant.

Our passage today is part of a final coaching session Jesus had with his disciples. They've been with him for three years but now they're worried because he's talking about leaving (14:1–5). The disciples need some reassurance and Jesus gives it to them in two ways:

Eventually, they will be with him. Someday Jesus will return for all those who have put their faith in him as the way to God and take them to a place prepared for them (14:3,6).

In the meantime, they can ask for his help. That promise (14:12–14) applies to you and me as well.

But the key to unlocking the mystery of Jesus' 'prayer guarantee' lies in two phrases that are easy to overlook. The first is 'in my name'. When we pray, we should ask for things that are consistent with what Jesus taught and did. That narrows down my prayer list. The second is 'bring glory to the Father'. When we pray, our focus should be on things that help more people understand who God really is. Those are the kind of prayers that get results.

APPLY How has prayer changed you?

PRAY Can you pray about something right now that will bring glory to the Father – that is, that demonstrates real trust in him and his character?

74

Serious forgiveness

Date: *The hard sayings of Jesus*

PRAY   Begin your time with God today by praying the Lord's
             Prayer slowly, phrase by phrase.

READ   Matthew 18:15–35

REFLECT

*This is how my heavenly Father will treat each of you unless you forgive
your brother from your heart.* Forgiveness is one of the toughest aspects
of maintaining healthy relationships. Just ask someone who's married!
But forgiveness was essential to Jesus' message and mission and it's
the theme of this passage.

Jesus begins by explaining a very practical method for resolving
conflict (18:15–20). First, talk to the person… privately; then go with
others; and then involve the church. As a last resort, the relationship
must be put on hold, remembering that Jesus was always willing to
accept sinners who repented.

Sadly, not many people have ever followed Jesus' advice. Counsellors
today talk about 'triangulation'; that's when we talk to a third party
instead of directly to the person who's offended us. It can be just a
fancy name for gossip and it's deadly in a church.

In response to Jesus' forgiveness formula, Peter asks a question
(18:21) that might be put something like this: 'Lord, when is it okay to
hate my brother and get revenge?' What Peter is fishing for is a time
limit on when he can stop forgiving. I can just imagine Jesus shaking
his head and chuckling, 'You know, Peter, if you have to ask how many
times you should forgive, you just don't get it.' When we really come to
understand how much God has forgiven us, there's no question: we
must *always* be willing to forgive those who offend us.

But all that sets up one of the most challenging statements Jesus ever
made (18:35). Could it really be that God gets angry with us if we
don't forgive? Apparently so. Those who have been forgiven a large
debt should be the most generous towards others. That's the whole
point of the parable (18:23–34). What Jesus is saying is that our
heavenly Father is serious about forgiveness and we must be too.

APPLY   How can you make receiving the forgiveness that Jesus
             offers an ongoing experience in your life?

PRAY   Bring to mind one person with whom you have a broken
             or strained relationship. Ask God to show you what he
             wants you to do in order to make things better.

75

Date:

Get serious

PRAY   Lord, help me to follow you more closely today.

READ   Mark 8:31 – 9:1

REFLECT

If anyone would come after me, he must deny himself and take up his cross and follow me. This is one of the most misunderstood statements Jesus ever made.

How many times have you heard someone sigh and say in reference to some minor irritation, 'Well, we all have our cross to bear, don't we?' But, for Jesus, taking up his cross was not just a coping mechanism. It was a symbol of all-out obedience to his Father's will. He was on his way to die.

Let's back up for a minute. Peter has just stumbled into one of his greatest 'Aha!' moments; he's finally come out with who Jesus really is (8:29). You'd think Peter would get a gold star for his answer.

Instead, Jesus gives a serious lecture; he teaches the disciples (8:31) and then rebukes Peter (8:33). Why? Because although they could now say the right things about Jesus they still didn't understand who he was; they viewed him from a human rather than divine perspective.

That presents a challenge for us today. Those of us who are surrounded by Christian teaching – in churches, sermons, books and so on – can quickly learn to say the right things about Jesus without understanding what they mean. True understanding comes when we put into practice the things Jesus said and did.

That's part of what Jesus meant by saying, 'Follow me'. Jesus gave up his rights as the Son of God to die for the sins of the world. For us, following Jesus will mean that the focus of our lives will no longer be the pursuit of happiness. Rather it will be to draw closer to Jesus and to become more single-minded about sharing him with others by our words and actions (8:35). We must die to our own agenda and live for Jesus' agenda.

APPLY   How would you describe the focus of your life? In what ways have you taken up your cross to follow Jesus?

PRAY   Father, I find it so easy to focus on the things of this world and so difficult to focus on the things that matter most to you. Please help me to live with your priorities today.

DISCUSSION QUESTIONS: THE HARD SAYINGS OF JESUS

After you've completed the five readings in this section, get together with another person or group to talk about the things you've learned. Begin by sharing the insights you gained from your own reflection on the passages. Then use the following questions to help you continue the conversation.

1   Of all the things Jesus said (both those mentioned in this section and others you may have read in the Gospels), which are the most difficult for you to understand? To obey? Why?

2   Was there ever a time in your life when you were moving 180 degrees away from God? What was it like? How did you turn around?

3   Have you ever experienced a specific answer to your prayers? What happened and how did it affect your relationship with God?

4   Have you ever failed to receive an answer to a specific prayer? What happened and how has it affected your view of God and prayer?

5   How do you usually resolve conflicts with people who have offended you?

6   Which is a bigger priority for you – pursuing happiness or following Jesus? What evidence can you offer?

THE CRUCIFIXION OF JESUS

The cross of Jesus Christ has become the most recognised and copied symbol in the world. Today it's a popular fashion statement whose original meaning has become lost to many people who wear it or display it.

But in our next five readings, we'll go back and examine what the Bible says about the crucifixion of Jesus. As you'll see, it's not a pretty picture. The events that led to the death of Jesus were completely unfair and out of control; at least that's how it seemed from a human point of view. Jesus was betrayed by Judas and then deserted by all the disciples. He was arrested and denied any sense of due process of law. At the Jewish trial, the bias and hatred of his accusers were obvious. And, at the Roman trial, the judge knew Jesus was innocent but condemned him to die anyway.

Worst of all, crucifixion was perhaps the most gruesome form of execution ever imagined. At the time of Jesus it was used in the Roman Empire as a way not only of punishing but also of humiliating enemies of the state. Victims were stripped naked and whipped to a bloody pulp, then made to carry the wooden beams on which they would be hanged. Modern medical experts suggest that death could occur from any number of causes including shock to the body, loss of blood, or simply suffocation as the weight of the victim's own body hanging from the cross cut off oxygen to the lungs. And the process could take hours or days to run its course. Any way you look at it, crucifixion was a horrible way to die.

One thing you'll want to keep your eye on in this section is the way Jesus reacted to the nightmare of his arrest, trials and crucifixion. Even though he was the victim, he often seems in control of events. That's because the cross was the reason he had come to earth. He also seemed more concerned about others than he was about his own pain and suffering; especially note the things he said while he hung on the cross.

Finally, because the story of Jesus' crucifixion has been told hundreds of time in plays, movies and books, you'll want to pray about two things. First, ask God to help you see and experience these familiar passages in a fresh, new way. And second, ask God to help you understand why Jesus allowed himself to be crucified.

76   **Busted!**

Date: *The crucifixion of Jesus*

PRAY   Lord Jesus, I'm about to walk with you through the most difficult part of your life on earth. As I do, please give me a better understanding of why you did it.

READ   Matthew 26:47–56

REFLECT

Over the years, scholars have speculated as to why Judas betrayed Jesus. Some say he was disillusioned; he lost faith that Jesus could ever become a political superstar for Israel. Others say he was greedy; 30 pieces of silver was an offer no thief could refuse (John 12:4–6). Still others say he was impatient; he wanted to force Jesus into action – like giving Popeye a can of spinach as the bad guys close in.

The truth is, we don't really know what motivated Judas to do what he did. We do know that his act of betrayal was no accident; it was intentional. Judas planned exactly how he would stab his master in the back (26:48,49). Perhaps the most baffling thing about Judas' charade is that he thought he could get away with it. But don't we do the same thing today? It's no good acting as though we love Jesus while cultivating a heart full of sin (Jeremiah 17:9). Jesus saw through Judas and he sees through us.

How incredible then that Jesus still called Judas his 'friend' (26:50). Even though he knew what was about to happen, Jesus offered Judas one last opportunity to change his mind. In fact, Jesus had been giving Judas opportunities to change course throughout the Gospel accounts. The real tragedy for Judas was not this single, dramatic act of betrayal. Rather, it was the accumulation of many little acts of betrayal that led to his final rejection of the Saviour.

But perhaps the most striking thing about this passage is Jesus' confidence. Even though he could easily stop Judas and his posse dead in their tracks (26:53), Jesus allowed himself to be arrested without a fight; he didn't demand to see a lawyer and he didn't even scream for help when the rest of the disciples cut and ran (26:56). That's because his highest priority wasn't to save his own skin; it was to fulfil the mission God had given him (26:54,56). He willingly gave up his life for the sins of the world (John 10:17,18).

APPLY   What might it mean to betray Jesus today?

PRAY   Lord Jesus, I'm sorry for all the little ways I turn my back on you. Please let me experience your embrace and friendship today.

77

Kangaroo court

Date: *The crucifixion of Jesus*

PRAY   Living God, I ask you to give me a clearer understanding
              of Jesus as 'the Christ, the Son of God' as I read and pray
              today.

READ   Matthew 26:57–68

REFLECT

As a young man, I got a ticket for jumping a red light. Because I
believed the light was amber, I decided to appeal in court. As I waited
my turn to stand before the magistrate, I watched as one by one other
defendants lost their appeal. They were led away to pay their fines on
the spot. I suddenly panicked; there was no money in my wallet. I was
at the mercy of the court.

In our passage today, Jesus was at the mercy of this Sanhedrin court –
only the stakes were much, much higher. Not only that, Caiaphas and
his cronies were breaking all the rules of due process. First, the trial
took place at night instead of during the day. Second, the charges were
based on false evidence (26:59) and false witnesses (26:60). But the
greatest flaw was that the judge and jury had already made up their
minds; they were looking for an excuse to execute Jesus (26:59).

The sad truth is, when a person makes up their mind to reject Jesus,
no amount of evidence will cause them to change. Ultimately,
accepting Jesus involves both a change of mind and a change of heart.

But what exactly caused Caiaphas and the teachers of the Law to act
more like a gang of thugs than the respected leaders that they were?

Jesus had shown disrespect for the Temple (26:61,62). That's what the
religious leaders thought, and it's a chilling reminder not to let our
religious institutions become more important than following Jesus.

Jesus claimed to be the Son of God (26:63,65). Caiaphas rightly
identified that as the central issue. He was unwilling to accept Jesus on
that basis – and that's the biggest mistake anyone can ever make.

I'm glad to say that when I stood in the court years ago the magistrate
accepted my side of the story and let me go. I left the courtroom
relieved and happy. But that pales into insignificance compared to the
joy I feel knowing that Jesus willingly accepted the unfair verdict of
this kangaroo court so that he could pay the debt of sin for you and
me.

APPLY   Have you ever had a change of heart and mind about
              Jesus? When and why?

PRAY   Pray for one person you know who's decided not to
              believe in Jesus.

78   Courtyard debacle

           The crucifixion of Jesus

PRAY   'Our God, you bless everyone whose sins you forgive and wipe away. You bless them by saying, "You told me your sins, without trying to hide them, and now I forgive you"'(Psalm 32:1,2, CEV).

READ   Matthew 26:69 – 27:10

REFLECT

When I was in high school I had a good friend who was Jewish. His house contained symbols of his family's active participation in Judaism; sometimes he'd even try to teach me Hebrew phrases. One day he was visiting my house and saw symbols of our family's active participation in the Christian faith and said, 'You think the Messiah has come, but we're still waiting for him.' Instead of telling him about Jesus, I replied rather weakly, 'Well, that's where our two religions differ.' To this day I regret the lost opportunity; it felt to me almost like a denial of Jesus.

That's why this account of Peter's famous denial always gets to me; I've done it too. I'm particularly sobered by the progression of Peter's failure. His first denial is that of a double agent (26:70); perhaps he said it just to stay inside the enemy's camp. Then, in the face of mounting pressure, he denies Jesus with greater emphasis (26:72); it's becoming easier. When Peter is cornered and forced to declare where he stands with Jesus, he erupts with a final, angry denial (26:74); it's as if he'd been practising for this moment all night long.

The good news, as we'll see in a future reading, is that Jesus used this courtyard debacle to strengthen Peter's faith and empower him for a new future of productive ministry (John 21:15–19). If we are willing to repent of denying Jesus and sinning against him, no failure is so great that it can separate us from God or keep us from serving him.

Tragically, Judas never understood that. Although he felt deep remorse (27:3), he never came to the place of repenting. But the fact is, there was hope for him even at this final hour. Like the thief on the cross, Judas could have called out to Jesus (Luke 23:39–43) and been forgiven. Ironically, there was less hope for the chief priest and elders whose unbelievable hypocrisy and arrogance (27:4–10) sealed their fate.

APPLY   What are some ways you have denied Jesus? What are some ways you could stand up for him?

PRAY   Ask God to forgive you for any ways you have denied him and ask him for the courage to stand up for Jesus at the next opportunity.

79

Date:

It's all about you, Jesus

PRAY   Father, you know the concerns of my heart today. Please show me what I most need to hear today from your Word.

READ   Luke 22:66 – 23:25

REFLECT

Some time ago I had lunch with two close friends who were curious about my faith in Jesus. They asked several good, honest questions and I was encouraged by the direction of our discussion. But after a while the conversation took a turn; my friends were alarmed at the way religion and politics often got mixed up together in public debate. As a result, they had difficulty separating my commitment to following Jesus from a particular political agenda.

That's exactly what's happening in our reading today; political concerns have overwhelmed true religion. Notice the spin the religious leaders put on their accusations of Jesus: 'He's undercutting our national security, he opposes your taxes policy and he's planning a political takeover' (my paraphrase of 23:2). It's all about politics. Thank God there are some political leaders who are attempting to govern today based on their deeply-held spiritual values. But God save us from leaders who use those values for political gain. It's a fine line, and getting it wrong prevents people from hearing the good news.

Our passage also gives us two examples of religion and politics gone awry. *Herod* was interested in Jesus, but only for entertainment (23:8); politicians always want to be near celebrities. Jesus made it clear that he was no celebrity entertainer (23:9); we must accept him as Lord and Saviour or not at all. But perhaps the most famous example came on the watch of *Pilate*, the man who sentenced Jesus to death. Part of him wanted to do the right thing (23:13–17,20–22) but in the end he didn't believe there was any such thing as truth (John 18:38) and it caused him to reject the ultimate source of Truth. Some say that is an apt analogy of our modern society.

Christians need to be careful not to misuse faith issues in politics or, worse, to politicise the mission of the Church. That's why I am moved every time I sing the Matt Redman song about worship: 'I'm sorry Lord for the thing I've made it, when it's all about you, it's all about you, Jesus.'

APPLY   How do your religious beliefs shape your political views?

PRAY   Lord, reveal to me any ways that my viewpoint is at odds with your heart and your Word.

80   Remember me

The crucifixion of Jesus

PRAY   'Remember not the sins of my youth and my rebellious
              ways; according to your love remember me, for you are
              good, O LORD' (Psalm 25:7).

READ   Luke 23:26–56

REFLECT

Whenever I read this passage, I have a sense that I'm on holy ground;
the crucifixion of Jesus is the most amazing demonstration of
sacrificial love the world has ever seen. Over the years, movie-makers
have done their best to depict what it must have been like, but no one
can ever fully know the extent of the suffering Jesus endured. And yet,
for all the physical pain, the worst part for Jesus was that God
temporarily abandoned him; the Father turned his back on his
beloved Son (Matthew 27:45,46). That's what it took to make a way
for you and me and the entire human race to be forgiven our sins and
restored to God.

What amazes me now about this account is that even in the midst of
his excruciating ordeal, Jesus was more concerned about others than
himself. To the women mourning him, Jesus offered a prophetic
warning (23:27–31); he wanted them to be prepared for the hard
times that would follow his death. To the people, leaders and solders
who mocked him, Jesus offered forgiveness (23:34), whether they
realised they needed it or not. To the angry thief, Jesus offers silence
(23:39); he doesn't try to retaliate. And to the repentant thief, Jesus
more than offers – he promises – paradise (23:43).

During my 13 years on the staff of Prison Fellowship, I had the
opportunity to go into prison many times with Chuck Colson. Often
Chuck preached to the inmates from this passage with the message
that it's never too late to turn back to Jesus and accept his forgiveness
for sin. Many inmates gave their lives to Christ as a result of that
simple appeal.

In a very real sense, this passage offers us the defining picture of what
the **EssentialJESUS** is all about, whether we're behind bars or out in
the world. Because of our sin, all of us are condemned to die; we're
either one thief or the other. The real question is how we will respond:
with insults (23:39) or with a heartfelt 'Remember me' (23:42)?

APPLY   Take time to put yourself in this story. What do you think
              and feel as you imagine yourself at the foot of the cross?

PRAY   Spend a few minutes humbly thanking Jesus for what he
              endured for you on the cross.

DISCUSSION QUESTIONS: THE CRUCIFIXION OF JESUS

After you've completed the five readings in this section, get together with another person or group to talk about the things you've learned. Begin by sharing the insights you gained from your own reflection on the passages. Then use the following questions to help you continue the conversation.

1   Have you ever known, or known of, someone who has completely turned their back on Jesus? What caused them to do this?

2   Is anyone so evil that they lose the opportunity to repent? Do you think Judas had a chance to change his mind?

3   Have you ever hidden your true beliefs about Jesus? Why and how?

4   Have you ever been bold about your faith at a time when you felt pressure to hide it? What happened and how did you feel afterwards?

5   Do you think politicians should talk about their religious beliefs? And govern based on their religious beliefs? Why/ why not?

6   What are the best examples today of how religion and politics should mix? And bad examples?

7   Imagine a person who's never heard of Jesus. How would you explain the crucifixion in a way that person would understand?

THE RESURRECTION OF JESUS

Even people who don't consider themselves churchgoers will often attend services at Christmas and Easter. As a result, just about everyone knows at least two stories about Jesus: his birth and his resurrection.

What we'll do in our next five readings is cover all the major passages in the Bible about the resurrection. First we'll look at the four Gospel accounts and you'll find it fascinating to go through them back to back, spotting the similarities in them. Each Gospel writer, though, captured different details and nuances of what happened. Matthew told his story by intertwining experiences of four separate people. Mark emphasises the power that was unleashed by the resurrection. Luke adds an extended account of an encounter that two disciples had with the resurrected Jesus. And John highlights the restoration of the relationship between Peter and Jesus. It's sort of like having four newspaper reporters covering the same event. When we put all the accounts together, we get a pretty complete picture of what happened.

In our fifth reading, we'll look at what the early Church leader Paul taught about the resurrection many years after it happened. By then, the first-century Christians were beginning to have doubts about whether the resurrection of Jesus even happened or not, or whether it was all that important after all. So Paul wrote to reassure the doubters and to firmly re-establish the importance of the resurrection.

As you go through this section, think about what parts of the account stand out to you? Which facts seem most convincing to you? And how could you explain your view of the resurrection to someone who wasn't sure about it?

81

Resurrection thriller

The resurrection of Jesus

PRAY   Lord Jesus, I want to come and see for myself what happened in that tomb. Please give me new insights into the truth about your resurrection.

READ   Matthew 28

REFLECT

I love good spy novels and thrillers; I read them in bed at night or when I'm pedalling on the exercise bike at the YMCA gym. One of the things that appeals to me about these books is that often they intertwine several separate plotlines in short chapters that all come together in the end. That's exactly how Matthew constructed his account of the resurrection of Jesus.

Plot 1 – the basic report, told with dramatic detail (28:1–7) Note that the earthquake was violent; no wonder the guards were scared stiff. The angel had a dazzling appearance but assumed a casual position, sitting on the stone. It's as if he was saying, 'What's the big deal; Jesus told you this would happen, right?'

Plot 2 – the reaction of the two Marys (28:8–10) They are overwhelmed with conflicting emotions of fear and joy. Even so, the angel gives them a threefold command: don't be afraid, come and see, go and tell – good marching orders for any follower of Jesus. For the two Marys it led to a life-changing encounter with Christ.

Plot 3 – the 'bad guys' (28:11–15) The religious leaders, aware of the disastrous PR implications if word got out that Jesus actually did rise from the dead, paid the guards to spread disinformation about what happened.

Plot 4 – the motivational conclusion (28:16–20) These verses are often called the great commission because in them Jesus empowered his followers to share the gospel with the whole world. But the most inspirational aspect is not a vision of worldwide evangelism. Rather, it's the reality that Jesus will be with his followers for ever.

APPLY   Do you ever feel that Jesus is really with you? When?

PRAY   Father, I'm so thankful for the empty tomb. Help me to overcome my fears so I can tell others about your Son, Jesus.

82

Gospel power

Date: *The resurrection of Jesus*

PRAY   Heavenly Father, 'I want to know Christ and the power of his resurrection' (Philippians 3:10). Show me how that's possible today as I read your Word.

READ   Mark 16

REFLECT

Perhaps your Bible includes a note indicating that most early manuscripts don't include Mark 16:9–20. What's that all about? Over the years, scholars have offered different explanations but the most likely is that either Mark died just before he finished his Gospel account, or the last section of his scroll was somehow destroyed and, as a result, someone close to Mark filled in the last section. We'll never know for sure but over the centuries the Church has agreed on this: these verses are still part of the inspired Word of God.

So what do we learn from this account of the resurrection? First, we note the many similarities to other Gospel accounts, a fact that enhances the credibility of this passage. Mark reports that the resurrection was discovered by the women close to Jesus, early on the Sabbath, and that an angel (described as a young man) was present to explain things. And note the angel's message is virtually the same as we read in Matthew (compare Matthew 28:5–7 with Mark 16:6,7). Everyone has the same basic story. But our reading today gives us two unique insights into this momentous day:

There are consequences of our choices about the gospel. In this version of the great commission (16:15,16), Jesus' words are not just a motivational challenge but are linked to another of his 'hard sayings': our response to the good news determines whether we're 'saved' or 'condemned' (16:16). We must be very careful not to scare or manipulate people with these words. But, on the other hand, it's important to know there are consequences to anyone's decision about Jesus.

There is power in the message of the gospel. You may not feel comfortable with all the examples of power listed here (16:17,18); personally, I'm not a big fan of snakes! Again, we must be careful with these verses; we shouldn't sensationalise them or attempt dangerous things without clear direction from the Lord. But the fact remains: Jesus said we would do 'even greater things' after his death and resurrection (John 14:12). That's a powerful message.

APPLY   For you, what is the most powerful thing about the resurrection of Jesus? Why?

PRAY   Spend a few minutes asking God to show you how you could respond to the Great Commission in your world.

83   The third disciple

Date: *The resurrection of Jesus*

PRAY   Father, thank you that 'your word is truth' (John 17:17).
Open my eyes to see and understand that truth clearly
today...

READ   Luke 24:1–49

REFLECT

Some people enjoy looking for 'inconsistencies' in the Bible. For
example, Matthew reports there was one angel at the empty tomb
while Mark saw a young man. Luke says two men were present while
John says there were two angels. Inconsistencies? Hardly. What's clear
from all the descriptions is that these were angelic beings. And it's
perfectly reasonable to think that at different times there were either
one or two present. Hyperventilating over the details of the
resurrection accounts can cause us to lose sight of the main point:
Jesus was no longer in the tomb.

The unique feature of Luke's account is the report of Jesus'
appearance to the two disciples on the road to Emmaus (24:13–35).
We can easily imagine the shock and discouragement these men were
feeling. For the past three years they'd been on a wild ride with Jesus
as he preached the good news, healed the sick and confronted the
religious leaders. But they didn't understand who Jesus really was;
they thought he was a prophet destined to become Israel's political
saviour (24:19–21). So when he died, they concluded it was 'game
over' for Jesus and for Israel.

We can also feel the frustration in Jesus' response to these two
followers: 'Guys, you've missed the whole point!' Jesus wasn't the
leader of a political movement; people still have that misconception
today. He was 'the Christ', the one God had promised to send in order
to save humankind from sin (24:26). And the way he would
accomplish that is through suffering, death and resurrection.

Wouldn't you love to have been part of this private Bible study with
Jesus (24:27)? In a sense, you are! As you discover for yourself 'what
was said in all the Scriptures' about the essential Jesus, it's as if you are
'the third disciple' on the road to Emmaus. And my prayer is that
you'll come to the same conclusion as the others: 'It is true!' (24:34).

APPLY   What misconceptions about Jesus do people have today?
How does that inform how you share the truth about
Jesus?

PRAY   Pray for one person you know who is confused about
who Jesus really is.

84

Follow me!

The resurrection of Jesus

PRAY   Prayerfully think of the pressures and stresses you face
             today. Imagine that you are handing each one to Jesus...

READ   John 20:1 – 21:25

REFLECT

There are many good ways to get a better understanding of the Bible's
message. One way is to develop a daily 'quiet time' – that is, to read a
short Bible passage prayerfully each day and then reflect on how to
live it out. Another is to read through the Bible in a year; another is to
conduct an in-depth study of a single Bible book. Our reading today
presents us with yet another option: studying the characters in the
Bible. John reports on the resurrection of Jesus by describing how
different people reacted to this significant event.

Mary Magdalene was a woman Jesus had cured of demon-possession
(Mark 16:9; Luke 8:2). John and all the other Gospel writers report
she was the first one to the tomb that morning. Often a person who
has been forgiven much will become an especially committed follower
of Jesus.

Thomas will forever be remembered for his doubts (20:19–31). But I
believe he also deserves credit for his honesty. Others had questions
about Jesus' resurrection (20:9), but Thomas was the only one with
the guts to admit them and to change his mind publicly when
presented with the truth (20:28).

Peter – one of the disciples Jesus had groomed for leadership – had
failed Jesus big time in his hour of need (Matthew 26:69–75). It's
significant that Peter must re-affirm his love for Jesus three times
(21:15–19), matching his three denials. Once their relationship is
restored, Jesus takes Peter back to the very first words he ever said to
him, 'Follow me' (21:19; Matthew 4:19). It's as if Jesus is saying, 'If
you want to be a leader, you must first understand what it means to be
my follower.'

John himself is the fourth character in this passage. Although he tries
not to attract attention, it's clear he has developed a special
relationship with Jesus (20:2; 21:7,20–24), and a firm belief in the
truth of his resurrection (20:8). The two go hand in hand.

APPLY   Which of the four characters in this passage do you
             identify with the most? Why?

PRAY   Lord, I admit that I have doubts and failures. Even so, my
             greatest desire is to be your committed follower. Show
             me how to do that today.

85

Fact and hope

The resurrection of Jesus

PRAY   Father, as I read and reflect on these words today, give me a deeper experience of the living Jesus.

READ   1 Corinthians 15

REFLECT

This is part of a letter written by Paul to the church in a city named Corinth. It had been several years since Jesus' death, and people were beginning to ask tough questions: Did his resurrection actually happen? Does it really matter if it did or not? If it did, what significance does it have for us now? Have you ever asked any of those same questions?

So how did Paul answer? He starts by giving his account of the resurrection (15:3–8) which includes all the facts we discovered in the four Gospels. Although Paul didn't go to the empty tomb himself that morning, he did have an encounter with the resurrected Jesus some time later (Acts 9:1–19). He also had another reliable source of information, one that is still available to us today: he studied the Scriptures (15:3,4). That's the best way to answer our questions about Jesus. Paul addresses two key issues:

The historical fact of the resurrection (15:12–34) That's still a big issue today. Some want to 'deconstruct' the Bible; others want to 're-interpret' what it says: 'Well... whether the tomb was empty or not isn't important. Just the idea of new life is inspirational.' 'Rubbish!' Paul shouts in response. Jesus was actually raised from the dead (15:20) and there were lots of eyewitnesses (15:5–8). Saying it didn't happen isn't inspirational; it's untrue and undermining of our entire faith (15:17–19). So cut it out!

The personal impact of the resurrection (15:35–58) In different ways, the Corinthians were asking, 'Okay, if there is such a thing as resurrection from the dead, how will affect me?' Paul does his best to describe our resurrection bodies (15:37–49) but, as he said earlier, 'now we see but a poor reflection' (1 Corinthians 13:12); we won't really know what it will be like until it happens. What we do know is that our spiritual bodies will be imperishable, glorious and powerful (15:42–44). That gives us a lot of hope – hope based on the fact of the resurrection (1 Peter 1:3).

APPLY   For you, what is the most important thing about the resurrection of Jesus?

PRAY   Father, increase my faith and hope in the fact of the resurrection of your Son, Jesus.

DISCUSSION QUESTIONS:
THE RESURRECTION OF JESUS

After you've completed the five readings in this section, get together with another person or group to talk about the things you've learned. Begin by sharing the insights you gained from your own reflection on the passages. Then use the following questions to help you continue the conversation.

1   How are you responding to the great commission Jesus gave his followers? How do you share the good news about Jesus in your world?

2   Do you remember your reaction the first time you heard about the resurrection of Jesus? How has your understanding changed over the years?

3   How would you respond to a church leader who said, 'You can still be a good Christian and not believe that Jesus was literally raised from the dead. It just doesn't square with what we know about science today'?

4   Have you ever had a major misunderstanding about something in the Bible? What was it? How can you know if your understanding of the Bible is correct now?

5   Do you have any lingering questions about the resurrected Jesus? What are they? Does the Bible have any answers?

THE EARLY CHURCH OF JESUS

When we moved back to Pennsylvania several years ago, our family had to find a new church. So for about a year we visited various congregations near our home. This gave us an opportunity to participate in a variety of Christian traditions and worship styles. I was encouraged to discover that there were many Christ-centred churches in our area.

Our search for a new church home also gave us a feel for the unique dynamics within each one. One church had great financial security but a small congregation and no full-time pastor. Another church had a great preacher with many full services on Sunday and lots of activities throughout the week – but it was such a busy place that we found it hard to connect with anyone. Another had a wonderful liturgy but the people didn't seemed interested, as if they were just going through the motions.

Our next section covers the first three chapters in the Book of Revelation, which is the record of a vision that John had nearly sixty years after the death and resurrection of Jesus Christ. In the vision it's as if Jesus himself has been a newcomer in seven first-century churches, and he describes the unique dynamics within each one. Imagine what Jesus would say if he visited your local church next Sunday!

Of the seven churches mentioned in Revelation, five fall into a 'good news/ bad news' category; Jesus commends them for some things but criticises them for others. Only two of the churches fall into an 'all good' category; Jesus praises them in spite of the fact that they are both facing severe struggles.

As you'll discover, some of the details in the Book of Revelation are difficult to understand. That's because it's the record of a vision. But concentrate on the main point. After all, when you wake from a dream, it's generally only the main point that you remember. And the main point of the next five readings is this: Jesus knows what's going on in the Church and he really, really cares. So let's get going, to see if we can piece together what Jesus thinks about *his* Church.

86   Vision for the emerging Church

Date: *The early Church of Jesus*

PRAY   Father, give me a clearer vision of your Son Jesus Christ as I read and pray today.

READ   Revelation 1

REFLECT

People sometimes refer to the last book of the Bible as 'John's Revelation'. But that's a little misleading because in fact, it is 'the revelation about Jesus Christ', as the opening sentence makes clear. What we need to understand as we begin our exploration of this challenging book is that although the writer John recorded this incredible vision, the Book of Revelation is all about Jesus.

And right away we notice the consistency between John's perspective and the rest of the New Testament. Jesus is *'the firstborn from the dead'* – he has been raised to everlasting life beyond physical death and we can experience that too (1:5; Colossians 1:15,18); he has freed us from sin *'by his blood'* – by paying the price a holy God required (1:5; Romans 5:9; Ephesians 1:7); his followers are *'a kingdom and priests'* – they can have a special and intimate relationship with God (1:6; 1 Peter 2:9); and someday Jesus will come again and *'every eye will see him'* (1:7; Philippians 2:9–11).

But John also gives us plenty of new information about Jesus.

He is majestic in appearance and his voice is powerful (1:12–15). When Jesus was on earth, John got as close to him as anyone (John 13:23–25). But, in this vision, John sees Jesus in all his heavenly glory. That contrast only highlights the miracle of the incarnation; in Jesus, the God of the universe became one of us.

He will decide who goes to heaven or hell (1:18). That's why we must take our decision about him very seriously. It will have eternal consequences.

He cares passionately about the Church (1:11). Jesus has something to say about the emerging Church of the first century (1:11). It reminds us that he knows and cares what goes on in our churches too, which is a sobering thought.

APPLY   How do you view Jesus – as majestic and powerful or close and friendly?

PRAY   Spend a few minutes thanking Jesus for the things you learned about him in this passage.

87

Faithful or unfaithful?

Date: *The early Church of Jesus*

PRAY   Lord, there are lots of things that get in the way of my
             love for you. Help me to make a fresh start with you
             today as I read your Word.

READ   Revelation 2:1–11

REFLECT

During my adult life I've been a member of three different churches,
depending on where I worked and lived. As I think back, I realise they
were all different. Some had strong teaching; some didn't. Some were
active in the community; some weren't. Some had lots of people and
resources; some didn't. For a variety of reasons they all had their
strengths and weaknesses. That's the sense we'll get as we read Jesus'
assessment of the churches in the first century.

The church in Ephesus (2:1–7)   The good news about this body of
believers was that they were activists; they were willing to work hard
(2:2). Not only that, they were careful to avoid false teaching and even
suffered for their beliefs. The bad news was they'd forsaken their first
love, Jesus (2:4). They were like a husband who provides everything
his family needs but who is unfaithful to his wife. If there's not true
love for Jesus in the church, its members are just going through the
motions and Jesus doesn't like that. The way to rekindle dying love is
to repent and start again (2:5).

The church in Smyrna (2:8–11)   Smyrna was one of two that were
singled out for commendation only (the other is in Philadelphia, 3:7–
14). But, to the casual observer, this church may have looked like a
failure. They were poor, they were being criticised, and their members
were about to suffer persecution and imprisonment (2:8–10). That's
not such a great formula for church growth. Or is it? Today, places
where the Church around the world is facing the greatest persecution
is also where it is experiencing the fastest growth. That doesn't mean
we should throw our own churches into turmoil in an effort to boost
attendance. But it reminds us that when Christians stand strong for
the gospel, as they must in persecution, people will be attracted. Jesus
called that faithfulness (2:10) and that's what he wants to see in his
Church.

APPLY   What would it mean for you to stand strong for the
             gospel this week?

PRAY   Spend a few minutes praying for the churches you've
             been part of or come into contact with in your life.

88   'Hold on ... until I come'

Date: *The early Church of Jesus*

PRAY   Thank God for all the ways your involvement in the Church has helped you grow closer to him and to others.

READ   Revelation 2:12–29

REFLECT

I know people who have been searching for the perfect church all their lives. They evaluate the pastor, preaching and programmes wherever they attend, and then move on. It's important to find a church that loves Jesus and believes the Bible, and it may take some finding. But, as Groucho Marx once said, 'I refuse to join any club that would have me as a member.' Churches aren't perfect because they're made up of imperfect people.

The two churches in our reading today certainly weren't perfect:

The church in Pergamum (2:12–17) These believers had a wonderful history: they had remained true to Jesus during a period of unusual stress and persecution (2:13). But that spiritual victory was long past; now they were being enticed by false teaching (2:14,15). There are churches and denominations today that have a wonderful history of evangelism and outreach but who have lost their commitment to the gospel and biblical teaching. As a result, they are gradually dying. Jesus says the way to fix that situation is straightforward: 'Repent!' (2:16).

The church in Thyatira (2:18–29) They were a loving, faithful, serving and persevering congregation (2:19). What pastor wouldn't be happy with that? But the church in Thyatira had the same problem as Pergamum: they were tolerating false teaching (2:20). And notice that it led to immoral behaviour. When human reason takes a higher place than biblical principles the Church begins to look no different than the world. For example, a recent survey found that Bible-believing Christians were just as likely to divorce as non-Christians.

All this raises an important question: how do we live with the fact that there's no perfect church? Jesus says, 'Hold on to what you have until I come' (2:25). In other words, remain faithful to the gospel and God's Word and eagerly look forward to his return. We can do that no matter what church we belong to.

APPLY   What would Jesus say about your church? And your contribution to it?

PRAY   Lord, you know the church isn't perfect and neither am I. Even so, help me to hold firmly to the gospel and to look eagerly for your return.

89   The dead church

Date: *The early Church of Jesus*

PRAY   Father, I want to be 'dead to sin' but 'alive to God' (Romans 6:11). Please show me how I can do that today.

READ   Revelation 3:1–13

REFLECT

Years ago I attended an urban church that some of my friends thought was dead. It was part of a denomination that was drifting away from the Bible. The church was located in a difficult neighbourhood and we struggled to maintain a large stone building that hadn't been filled in 50 years. But a small group of us began meeting in a side chapel once each week to pray for the church. As a result, God did a wonderful thing: he didn't suddenly fill the pews, but he made those of us who prayed spiritually alive.

The church in Sardis (3:1–6) This was the reverse of that urban church I attended. It had 'a reputation of being alive' (3:1). Today, everyone wants to be part of a successful church. Mega-churches attract the best preachers, the most money and the largest congregations. But is that what Jesus wants? Not necessarily. Even though the church in Sardis had everything going for it, Jesus considered it dead. Why? Because its members weren't fully obeying the basic teachings of the gospel (3:2,3). That can happen if we focus on a few 'precious promises' but aren't committed to reading and applying all parts of the Bible, for example. Without that, Jesus says to the church in Sardis, 'you are not completely obeying God' (3:2, CEV).

The church in Philadelphia (3:7–13) Like the church at Smyrna, these believers didn't look successful; they were weak and facing opposition (3:8,9). But they got the main things right: 'You obeyed my word and did not deny me' (3:8, NLT).

Perhaps the most encouraging thing from this passage is that whether you find yourself in a dead church or one that is truly alive, Jesus says you will 'walk with me' (3:4) if you remain faithful to him and his Word. The best reason to read and live out the full message of the Bible is not so that we can be 'holier than thou'; it's so that we can be closer to Jesus.

APPLY   Do you think Jesus would consider your church dead or alive? Why?

PRAY   Spend this time praying for your church and for all the churches near where you live.

90

Lukewarm for God

Date: *The early Church of Jesus*

PRAY 'Praise be to God, who has not rejected my prayer or withheld his love from me!' (Psalm 66:20).

READ Revelation 3:14–22

REFLECT

People who are passionate about God today are often labelled 'extremists'. A society that worships a valueless form of tolerance is threatened by anyone who knows what they believe and is willing to talk about it. Of course, we shouldn't try to cram our beliefs down the throats of others; that does more harm than good. But there's nothing wrong with making God our first priority; that's what he wants (Matthew 6:33).

The church in Laodicea (3:14–22)   No one would ever accuse the church in Laodicea of being a bunch of religious extremists; they were lukewarm for God, and that really bothered Jesus (3:15,16). Being lukewarm still bothers Jesus. For the Laodiceans, it was wealth that had dulled their passion for the things of God (3:17). Those of us who have material possessions should be thankful for what we have, but we should also heed this warning to the Laodiceans; it's impossible to love both God and money (Matthew 6:24). It's like trying to marry two people at the same time; it just doesn't work.

There are two other ideas in this passage worth pondering:

God wants us to repent (3:19). There is a connection between discipline and love. Sometimes we think that when bad things happen, God is out to get us. True, he's out to get us to repent, as Jesus makes clear. The fact is, God has an extreme love for us, so much so that he sent his Son to die for our sins (John 3:16; 1 John 4:9).

Jesus wants to be with us (3:20). This word picture communicates how much Jesus wants to be with us. When I was growing up, it seemed like every Sunday School classroom in the world had the same picture of a fair-haired Jesus knocking on a door in some garden. Those pictures may have been over-sentimental, but they taught me an important truth: Jesus is waiting for me to invite him into my life.

APPLY How would you characterise your relationship with Jesus right now – on fire, on ice or lukewarm?

PRAY What one way could you show your love for God this week, no matter what people think about you?

DISCUSSION QUESTIONS:
THE EARLY CHURCH OF JESUS

After you've completed the five readings in this section, get together with another person or group to talk about the things you've learned. Begin by sharing the insights you gained from your own reflection on the passages. Then use the following questions to help you continue the conversation.

1   If Jesus came to your church, what do you think he'd say? What message would Jesus have for the churches in your country?

2   Is it a good thing that, in general, the Western Church doesn't face much persecution? How can a congregation remain faithful when they live in peace and prosperity?

3   How can a church that's become large, wealthy and powerful keep Jesus as its first love? Do you know of any examples?

4   How can a person who's become successful keep Jesus as their first love? Do you know of any examples?

5   Do you think Christians today have become 'too tolerant' or 'too extreme'? Why/ why not?

6   If you find yourself in a dead church, how can you know whether to find a new church or stay and try to make things better? Have you ever been in this situation? What happened?

7   Have you ever felt lukewarm in your relationship with God? Have you ever been in a church that felt that way? What could you do to help your church 'stay awake'?

THE SECOND COMING OF JESUS

The Bible tells us that as Jesus was ascending into heaven after his death and resurrection, two angels appeared and said to the disciples, 'This same Jesus, who has been taken from you into heaven, will come back in the same way you have seen him go into heaven' (Acts 1:11). Ever since, the 'second coming' of Jesus has been eagerly anticipated by his followers in every age.

As early as the first century, however, questions began to emerge. Some people thought that the second coming had already occurred and that they had been left behind. Others thought that it would never happen and they mocked Christians who were still waiting. Still others used the confusion over the second coming to teach their own peculiar views of the end of the world. What's ironic is that all those things are still happening today.

That's why our next five readings are so useful; they'll help us clarify what the Bible says about this important topic. We'll begin by examining the ascension of Jesus; it's a preview of what his second coming will be like. Then we'll dig into the teachings of two key leaders in the early church – Paul and Peter – to find out how they answered the questions that were being raised. And finally, we'll take a look at Revelation 21 and 22, the last two chapters of the Bible, to get a picture of what the 'end times' will be like. And the encouraging thing is that the end is only the beginning of a new world with God at its centre!

But if the Bible is so clear about the second coming, why do so many still seem confused about it today? The answer, I believe, is that people take the information in the Bible to one of two extremes. Some make too much of the second coming; their whole worldview is built around the most obscure details of the end times. Others make too little of the second coming; for them, it might happen, it might not, but who cares?

That's why our goal in this section will be to form a balanced, biblical view of the second coming, because the Bible teaches beyond question that some day Jesus will come back in the same way that he went up into heaven. What a joyful day that will be!

91   The greatest sequel

Date: *The second coming of Jesus*

PRAY   Lord, 'guide me into all truth' about your death, resurrection, ascension and second coming.

READ   Acts 1:1–11

REFLECT

Have you ever watched a film that leaves you feeling there's definitely a sequel on the way? Perhaps the bad guy has been defeated but is still lurking out there somewhere. Or maybe the good guy has overcome his struggles and is now ready for a new adventure. In a sense, that's exactly what's happening in this passage. Luke, the writer of Acts, is setting up the greatest sequel of all time; he's preparing us for the second coming of Jesus Christ.

He does that by describing the dramatic conclusion to Jesus' life on earth. Luke had finished his Gospel account with a reference to the ascension of Jesus (Luke 24:50–53), but here he gives a fuller description of that unforgettable event. Note that he makes a point of reviewing the growing body of evidence for Jesus' resurrection (1:3–5). There were many, many eyewitnesses. But, for some, seeing is not always believing. Even after all the 'convincing proofs' (1:3), some still hadn't grasped the truth about Jesus. They couldn't get over their assumption that he was Israel's national hero (1:6).

We all bring assumptions to our consideration of Jesus. We get the truest picture of the essential Jesus by reading prayerfully what the Bible says about him. Earlier, Jesus taught that the Holy Spirit would help his followers understand the truth of the gospel after his death, resurrection and ascension (John 16:13). Now Jesus says the Holy Spirit will give his followers power for sharing that truth with a needy world (1:8).

But, as Jesus disappears into the clouds, it is the two angels who have the privilege of announcing the great sequel. Jesus 'will come back in the same way you have seen him go into heaven' (1:11). Just imagine if it happened today!

APPLY   If you knew Jesus was returning today or within the next 30 days, what difference would it make to your plans and priorities?

PRAY   Lord Jesus, I can hardly imagine what it will be like when you return. All I know is that I'm so thankful that you've made a way for me to be with you for ever.

92   'If I should die before I wake... '

Date: *The second coming of Jesus*

PRAY   Father, 'keep us in (your) grace, and guide us when perplexed; and free us from all ills, in this world and the next' (Martin Rinkart).

READ   1 Thessalonians 4:13 – 5:11

REFLECT

I read the newspaper almost every morning and I have a pattern for how I go about it. First I look at the front page, then sports, then news and editorials, then celebrity gossip. But there's one other thing I always check – the obituaries. For some reason I'm always curious about who's died. Admit it, you are too! People throughout the ages have been intrigued by the question: what happens to me after I die? That's exactly the question the believers in the first-century city of Thessalonica were pondering, and our reading today is Paul's answer to them.

He starts by reviewing the basic teaching of the gospel on this subject: those who believe that Jesus died and rose again can be certain that they'll enjoy eternal life with him (4:14,17). Paul then offers a succinct description of what Jesus' return will be like (4:16); it's a description that sounds very similar to others in the New Testament because it's based on the explanation Jesus himself gave (4:15; Matthew 24).

Paul then gives the Thessalonians two practical teachings to help them maintain a balanced understanding of the second coming:

Don't try to nail down dates and times (5:1). People are still distracted by that debate today, and the truth is only God knows when it will happen (Matthew 24:36). What we do know is that if we're not prepared, Jesus' return will take us by surprise; it could be like a 'thief in the night' (5:2).

Do spend time living for God in the present (5:4–8). This is good advice for us too. We are to put off the deeds of darkness and put on the lifestyle of those who live in the light, which sounds exactly like the advice Paul gave to believers (Ephesians 4:20–24).

The truth is, we'll always be curious about the second coming. But Paul reminds us that the most important thing to know is simply that we are ready for it.

APPLY   What is your answer to the question: what will happen to you after you die?

PRAY   Pray about the ways you could become more ready for the return of Jesus Christ.

93   **Don't be alarmed...**

Date: *The second coming of Jesus*

PRAY   'Be exalted, O God, above the heavens; let your glory be over all the earth' (Psalm 57:11).

READ   2 Thessalonians 2:1–12

REFLECT

Recently I was given a book written by a Christian author I hadn't come across. The first thing I did was look at the back cover to see the list of his other books. I was surprised to learn that one of his previous bestsellers was described as 'the definitive book on the afterlife'. Really? I thought *that* book was written a long, long time ago. It's called the Bible. Our reading from it today gives us more puzzle pieces for the picture of the second coming we've been putting together.

We learn here that some people were sensationalising the second coming, or simply spreading misinformation about it and, as a result, many believers worried they had been left behind (2:2). Paul says, 'Don't let anyone deceive you' and he proceeds to remind them of the basics: when Jesus returns, his followers will be with him. In other words, when it happens, you'll know.

But Paul tells us about some 'trigger' events to the second coming. There will be some kind of rebellion and the appearance of 'the man of lawlessness' (2:3). What in the world is he talking about? In different places throughout the Bible we find references to a final showdown between God and Satan; that's the rebellion. Also, during that final conflict, a key instrument of Satan called 'the Antichrist' will oppose God and be defeated (Matthew 24; Mark 13; Revelation 19:19–21; 20:7–10). Although Paul doesn't take time in this letter to explain everything, that's clearly what he has in mind.

So what does all this mean for us today? Simply this: we shouldn't become 'unsettled or alarmed' (2:2) if world events seem out of control. The Bible teaches that God will let things get worse before he steps in to fix it once and for all. But remember: we've already peeked at the end of the story – Jesus is coming back and that's all we really need to know.

APPLY   How does your understanding of the second coming of Jesus affect the way you react to world news today?

PRAY   Lord, this world would be a really scary place if I wasn't sure that you were coming back someday. Please show me how I can serve you best until that day.

94

Waiting for... ?

Date: *The second coming of Jesus*

PRAY   Father, when it comes to the second coming, sometimes I
              feel like this: 'I do believe; help me overcome my
              unbelief!' (Mark 9:24).

READ   2 Peter 3

REFLECT

I once saw a college production of *Waiting for Godot,* the famous play
by Samuel Beckett about two tramps, Vladimir and Estragon, who
spend the entire play anticipating the arrival of a person named
Godot. They talk, they have conflict, they meet other characters, but
in the end Godot never shows up. Although Beckett refused to explain
the play, his message was clear: life is meaningless if we spend it
waiting for something that never happens.

That's exactly how some first-century Christians were beginning to
feel about the second coming of Christ. They were waiting, waiting,
waiting... but nothing was happening. And, to make matters worse,
sceptics were becoming more vocal with their taunts (3:4). Today, over
2,000 years later, Jesus still hasn't returned. Have Christians been
misled into some meaningless play along with Vladimir and Estragon?

'Absolutely not!' is how Peter would answer, and he devotes the last
section of this letter to explaining why:

The biblical response First, Peter points to the words of the prophets
and the words of Jesus himself (3:2). Even though it's centuries later,
we have access to both in the Bible. People have always doubted God's
Word. So Peter reminds his readers that when God speaks, things
happen – like at creation and at the great flood in the time of Noah
(3:5,6). And, since God's Word says the second coming will happen,
we can be sure it will (3:7).

The philosophical response God is outside of time, says Peter (3:8); he
doesn't sit around marking his calendar as we do. As a result, what
seems like a long delay is actually a big opportunity for more people to
come to know him (3:15).

How then should we live as we wait for Jesus to return? We should
focus on living 'holy and godly lives' (3:11). Then we'll be drawing
closer and closer to Jesus while we wait for that day when we meet him
face to face (1 Corinthians 13:12).

APPLY   Do you ever have doubts about the second coming of
              Jesus? What are they, and what helps you overcome them?

PRAY   Lord, help me live a holy and godly life while I wait to
              meet you face to face someday.

95   Only the beginning

Date: *The second coming of Jesus*

PRAY   Father, as I near the end of my journey through the Bible, help me to get a clear understanding of the essential Jesus.

READ   Revelation 21:1 – 22:21

REFLECT

When I start reading a novel, I often turn to the back and scan the last few paragraphs first. Some people think that ruins all the fun, but I like to find out who will be left standing by the end of the story (shows you what kind of books I read!). In a sense, that's what we're doing in our passage today; the last paragraphs of the Bible give us a glimpse of the greatest happily-ever-after conclusion we could ever imagine.

As we've discovered, the Book of Revelation is a vision that John had a few decades after the resurrection (1:9,10). In the first three chapters, the focus was on specific messages from Jesus to seven first-century churches. In the last two chapters the focus has switched to the end of the world, and we discover that God intends to establish 'a new heaven and a new earth' (21:1). That's an encouraging thought when we consider what's happening in the world today.

There are probably a few things about this passage, like the rest of Revelation, that you find difficult to follow. Let me remind you again that, like in a dream, it's the main point that's most important rather than every little detail. And the main point is very clear. In the end, Satan is defeated (20:7–10), the curse of sin is broken (22:3) and God the Father and God the Son will be present with us: 'Look, the home of God is now among his people! He will live with them, and they will be his people. God himself will be with them' (21:3, NLT). What an incredible vision that is!

For those who belong to Christ, the end of the world is only a new stage of the eternal life begun when they first met him. That's the Bible's greatest story and that's at the heart of the **EssentialJESUS** story.

APPLY   How does God's plan to establish a new heaven and a new earth affect the way you live now?

PRAY   Lord, I look forward to the day when I'll see your face. Help me live my life with that end in mind. Come, Lord Jesus…

DISCUSSION QUESTIONS:
THE SECOND COMING OF JESUS

After you've completed the five readings in this section, get together with another person or group to talk about the things you've learned. Begin by sharing the insights you gained from your own reflection on the passages. Then use the following questions to help you continue the conversation.

1   How do you feel about the state of the world today? Does it seem worse, better or the same as it's always been? Explain your answer.

2   How would you respond to a friend who says, 'Look, after two thousand years I think it's safe to assume that Jesus *isn't* going to come back. Maybe Jesus meant it as a figure of speech rather than a literal promise'?

3   Have you ever run into a view of 'the end times' that doesn't seem to square with what the Bible says? How does it compare with what you learned in **EssentialJESUS**?

4   What's your rationale for making things better in the here and now when God is going to create a new heaven and a new earth anyway?

5   Some Christians say that, in light of the return of Christ, the only thing that matters is evangelism and that we shouldn't waste too much time on things like peace, justice, poverty and the environment. What do you say?

6   What is your view of heaven? What will it be like, who will be there and how can you be sure you'll be among them?

7   In what ways does your view of the second coming of Jesus affect the way you live today?

WHO IS JESUS TO YOU?

When I was growing up we had a tradition in our home that I didn't like very much. Each year on Good Friday, from noon until 3 pm, my mother would make me and my siblings go to our rooms and write out the answer to this question: Who is Jesus to you? I knew the reason she made us do this was because those were the hours that Jesus hung on the cross: 'It was now about the sixth hour, and darkness came over the whole land until the ninth hour' (Luke 23:44).

I didn't like it because at that time of the year it was just starting to get warm, and I always wanted to be outside playing baseball. And it seemed that on every Good Friday, the weather was perfect for baseball. But I'm glad she made us go to our rooms. Often, in spite of my grumpy attitude, when I finally sat down to write my answer, it became one of the most meaningful things I did all year.

I'm a grown man now, but I still take some time by myself on Good Friday and write in my journal about Jesus. I love to remind myself of how much he has done for me.

In our next section, you'll have an opportunity to examine the experiences of five people who had encounters with Jesus. The rich young man walked away from Jesus because he loved his money. Nicodemus didn't believe Jesus at first but, over time, he became a follower. Once the woman at the well got over her shame, she accepted Jesus as her saviour. Saul had a dramatic encounter with Jesus that changed his life – and the world – for ever. And Peter gave a stunning affirmation of Jesus even though he didn't yet understand all that it would cost him. But the thread that holds them all together is that each person had to make a personal decision about Jesus.

At the beginning of this book, I told you I'm a follower of Jesus but that your decision about him was your responsibility. I simply wanted to guide you through 100 Bible passages about Jesus and then leave it to you to come to your own conclusion. I'm still going to stick with that. But I will tell you this: my hope and prayer is that if you haven't yet made your decision to believe in Jesus and follow him, you will do so by the end of this book. If you'd like some help with that you can refer to *Beginning a relationship with Jesus Christ* on page 153.)

In writing this book, I've truly enjoyed taking a journey through the Bible's greatest story. And I hope that as you've read, reflected and prayed your way through the 100 stops on that same journey, you've not only gained an appreciation for who Jesus is, but you also developed a love for prayerfully reading God's Word. Don't let this be the end of your times with the Bible. Let it become the beginning of a lifetime of meeting God every day through the Bible and prayer.

96   The rich do-gooder

Date: *Who is Jesus to you?*

PRAY   Lord, clear my mind and heart of every distraction so that I can have a fresh encounter with you today.

READ   Matthew 19:16–30

REFLECT

Over the years, I've heard some people – usually those with lots of money – express frustration with this passage: 'Well, I guess we're all supposed to give away everything and live like Saint Francis, is that it?' I've also heard other people – usually those who wish they had more money – express satisfaction with this passage: 'Well, I guess rich people don't really understand the gospel, do they?' But a careful reading of what Jesus said reveals that he was talking not only about money and possessions, but also about something far more serious.

Notice that, in spite of all his wealth in this world, the rich man was worried about what would happen to him in the next. That's still the big issue. Regardless of who you are, what you know or even what you believe, at some point everyone must come to grips with this question: what happens to me after death?

The man in this passage thought he had it all figured out: do good things (19:16,20) and he would get a place in heaven. That's what many people believe today. They imagine a pair of giant scales in the cosmos, and if your good deeds outweigh your bad, then bingo, you're in! But Jesus pulls the rug out from under that perspective. First, he challenges what it means to be 'good' (19:17). He then carries the philosophy to its logical extension: just being good isn't good enough; to earn your salvation you must be perfect (19:21). Excuse me? Even the disciples were baffled; if a good, rich man can't get in, who can (19:25)?

By the end of the conversation Jesus made it clear there were two things preventing this man from gaining the eternal life he sought: his attachment to wealth and his belief that salvation could be earned through good works. The man went away sad because neither of those strategies works. In the end, Jesus made it clear that there is only one way to get to heaven: 'Follow me'. That means believing in Jesus and living like him – just what he had been saying all along.

APPLY   Are there things that prevent you from completely following Jesus? If so, what are they and what would it take to remove them?

PRAY   Spend a few minutes talking to Jesus, imagining that he has personally addressed this challenge to you: 'Follow me'…

97

Date: *Who is Jesus to you?*

PRAY   Lord, as well as knowing about you, please show me how
I can have a relationship with you as I read your Word
today.

READ   John 3:1–21

REFLECT

I've worked in non-profit organisations all my life and that's given me
many opportunities to try my hand at fundraising. I once telephoned a
man I had never met; I was hoping to begin a relationship that would
someday lead to a contribution. I had my phone script all prepared,
but before I got even a few seconds into it the man cut me off with,
'What's the bottom line; how much do you want?'

In a way, that's what Jesus does to Nicodemus; he cuts him off and
goes straight to the bottom line: you must be born again (3:3,7). Jesus
interrupted Nicodemus' theological script because he wanted to
address the real issue: in spite of his high position and religious
knowledge, Nicodemus was outside God's kingdom (3:3,5). It
reminds us that just going to church, or even knowing a lot about the
Christian faith, does no good unless we've been truly born again.

But what exactly does it mean to be 'born again'? Today, millions of
people claim they are. Some think of born-again Christians as
unpleasant zealots. In the US, some think of them as a voting block to
be manipulated. But Jesus defined them as people who believe that he
is the Son of God, the one who died on the cross to save humankind
from sin (3:14–18). And when a person finally accepts that truth, they
begin a whole new life.

That was a lot for Nicodemus to swallow all at once (3:9), and there's
no evidence here that he accepted Jesus' message. But the seed
planted that night began to grow; later Nicodemus defended Jesus
(John 7:50,51) and finally he identified himself publicly as a follower
of Christ (John 19:38–42). Some people put their trust in Jesus the
first time they hear the gospel message. For others, believing in Jesus
is a process with many steps. But no matter how it happens or how
long it takes, the bottom line is this: you must be born again.

APPLY   Where are you in the process of believing in Jesus?

PRAY   Spend a few minutes talking to Jesus, imagining that he
has personally addressed this challenge to you: 'You must
be born again'…

98

No more shame

Who is Jesus to you?

PRAY   'I sought the LORD, and he answered me; he delivered me
             from all my fears. Those who look to him are radiant;
             their faces are never covered with shame' (Psalm 34:4,5).

READ   John 4:1–42

REFLECT

The woman in our passage today was carrying more than just a water
jug as she walked to the well; her heart was burdened. How do we
know?

She was a Samaritan – a group of people ostracised by the Jews.

She was a woman – many at that time, including even the disciples,
would have considered her a second class citizen.

She had lived a sinful life – one that produced a series of broken
relationships (4:17,18).

No wonder she went to the well by herself in the heat of the day. Many
people today struggle with a deep sense of shame. Some can't forgive
themselves for a terrible sin in their past; others have been deeply
wounded by someone else's sin. Either way, sin and shame can leave
us feeling broken, unworthy and alone. But sometimes our lowest
moment is when we are closest to God (Psalm 34:18).

That's what happened to this woman. She met Jesus and he used the
encounter to change her life for ever. First he revealed that he was the
source of 'living water' (4:10,13,14); she probably thought he meant
'running water' from a moving stream. But he meant the Holy Spirit;
that's what Jesus offers to all who follow him. Next he told her that
soon everyone could have a relationship with God; everyone, not just
the Jews (4:22), would worship God in spirit and truth (4:23,24). But
this would only be possible because God's promised Messiah had
arrived (4:25,26).

By the end of the encounter, the woman accepted Jesus not just as a
man or as a prophet; she believed in him as 'the Saviour of the world'
(4:42). And that's what turned her burden of sin and shame into a
source of joy. She could invite her friends to meet the man 'who told
me everything I ever did' (4:29,39) because he had forgiven her. And
that joy is available to everyone who believes in Jesus today.

APPLY   How would you feel if you met someone who knew all
             your darkest secrets?

PRAY   Lord, you know everything I've ever done. I ask you to
             forgive me and then fill me with your living water.

99

Angry young man

Date:

Who is Jesus to you?

PRAY   Father, enable me to identify today one or two things I can do to draw closer to you.

READ   Acts 9:1–22

REFLECT

Saul was an angry young man (Acts 7:58). He hated Christians and tracked them down to throw them into prison. So much for religious tolerance. But Saul's vendetta raises an interesting question: Why does Jesus make some people so angry? For some it has to do with their unwillingness to give up a particular lifestyle. Others feel they've been betrayed by a Christian. Still others can't accept Jesus' claim to be the only way to God (John 14:6).

But often, all these reactions are a smokescreen for a deeper issue: external anger at Jesus can be a clue that an internal spiritual struggle is going on. That seems to be the case with Saul. There was no question about his passion for God. Elsewhere in the Bible we learn that he devoted his life to Judaism; he was a model Pharisee (Acts 22:3; 23:6). But when Saul literally 'saw the light' it burned off all his anger. He still had questions (9:5), but until he let go of the anger he couldn't hear the answers. That's true today as well.

I've heard some Christians apologise for the fact that, 'My testimony is not that dramatic', as if the only way to be truly converted is to get knocked to the ground and to hear the voice of Jesus.

Sometimes conversion is immediate and dramatic, and we can thank God for the times he chooses to work that way. But, more often, conversion is a gradual process where a person comes to faith in Jesus over time. Even Saul's conversion demonstrates this: he grew up in a religious environment, developed a passion for God, had a dramatic encounter with Jesus but then received support from the Christian community in Damascus (9:17–19). It took all these steps to transform the angry young man into God's chosen instrument who could preach that Jesus is the Son of God (9:15,20).

APPLY   What is the next step you could take in your relationship with Jesus?

PRAY   Ask God for the courage to take that next step.

100   The EssentialJESUS challenge

Date: *Who is Jesus to you?*

PRAY   Thank you, Father, for everything you've taught me during my journey through the Bible. Please show me anything else you want me to know.

READ   Luke 9:18–27

REFLECT

When I was in high school, our pastor invited me to share my testimony in front of the entire church. I agreed because I had grown up in a Christian home and I felt confident I knew what to say. But when the day finally arrived and I stepped to the front, I suddenly realised the challenge wasn't just to say what my pastor, or my parents, or anyone else wanted to hear. With the eyes of everyone staring at me, I had to say what I really believed about Jesus.

It's that kind of crunch moment that the disciples have reached in our reading today. As a result of Jesus' preaching, parables and miracles, everyone is talking about him. So Jesus asks a general question, 'Who do the crowds say I am?' (9:18). Most people today would be comfortable with that one; they could simply repeat what they've heard from others, which is exactly what the disciples did (9:19).

But Jesus didn't come to earth to help people memorise a textbook answer about him. He came so that everyone could have a personal relationship with him. So he presses the point; perhaps this is what he had been praying about earlier. 'Who do *you* say that I am?' (9:20). That's the **EssentialJESUS** challenge. And it is Peter, the impulsive fisherman, who rises to the challenge: 'You are the Christ, the Son of the living God' (9:20; Matthew 16:16). The disciples still had a lot to learn about Jesus, and a lot to go through with him (9:21–27). But they had crossed a threshold in their relationship with Jesus.

As I hope you've discovered in our journey through the Bible, what you believe about Jesus is the most important issue you'll ever face. And my prayer is that you'll join Peter and countless millions throughout the ages who have affirmed with all their hearts, 'You are the Christ, the Son of the living God', because when you do, you will have crossed the threshold into eternal life.

APPLY   What do you really believe about Jesus?

PRAY   Spend a few minutes talking to Jesus, imagining that he has personally addressed his challenge to you: 'Who do *you* say that I am?'...

DISCUSSION QUESTIONS:
WHO IS JESUS TO YOU?

After you've completed the five readings in this section, get together with another person or group to talk about the things you've learned. Begin by sharing the insights you gained from your own reflection on the passages. Then use the following questions to help you continue the conversation.

1   The rich young man rejected Jesus because he loved his money too much. How can we know when we've crossed that line – that we love money and possessions too much?

2   Jesus said you cannot serve both God and money (Matthew 6:24). How is that possible in our modern world?

3   For Nicodemus, coming to faith in Jesus was a process. What have been the steps in the process of your discovering who Jesus is? How long has it taken? What do you think the next step might be?

4   The woman at the well was struggling with her sense of shame. Have you ever felt as if negative experiences in your past were holding you up from drawing closer to God? What happened?

5   Early in his life, Saul was an angry person. Have you ever had a phase in your life when you've been angry with God? Why? Were you able to resolve the source of your anger? How?

6   Peter boldly declared his belief in Jesus. Have you ever been in a situation where you had to publicly explain what you believe about Jesus? What happened? Do you remember the first time you spoke up for Jesus?

7   Who is Jesus to you?

EssentialJESUS *notes*

EssentialJESUS *notes*

EssentialJESUS *notes*

EssentialJESUS *notes*

EssentialJESUS *notes*

EssentialJESUS *notes*

BEGINNING A RELATIONSHIP WITH JESUS CHRIST

As you've discovered in **EssentialJESUS**, the greatest story in the Bible is that God made a way for you to have a real relationship with him. That way is Jesus Christ. That may sound attractive to you. But, you may ask, 'How do I begin?' Here's how:

- *Admit* that you have sinned and that your sins have separated you from God.

- *Believe* that Jesus is the Son of God who died on the cross to pay for your sins and give you new life.

- *Decide* to follow Jesus for the rest of your life.

Here's a simple prayer that you might say to begin a lifelong relationship with Jesus.

> Dear God, I admit that I've done wrong things and that my sin has separated me from you. I believe you sent Jesus to earth to die for the sins of the world – including mine – and that you brought him back to life again. Lord Jesus, from now on, I'm deciding to follow you every day. Holy Spirit, I ask for your help to live a new life. Amen!

About your new life

When you begin a relationship with God, you'll want to make it grow. Here are some ideas for deepening your relationship with God:

Talk to God. That means prayer. You can talk to God at any time, either silently or out loud. God loves to hear from you.

Listen to God. The best way is by reading the Bible; you'll come to know God better and understand how he wants you to live.

Join a church. You need the support of other believers. Find a church where the people love Jesus and believe the Bible... and you'll begin to grow.

God bless you!

Whitney T Kuniholm

BIBLE READING – WHAT NEXT?

Scripture Union is in the business of helping people read the Bible and pray so that they make and grow a personal relationship with God.

You can call us to **request free back issues** from our range of quarterly personal Bible reading guides. We publish several different guides, each with their own character, and our staff will be glad to advise you as to which would be most suitable for you to try.

- DAILY BREAD aims to help you enjoy, explore and apply the Bible, with practical comments to help you relate it to everyday life.
- CLOSER TO GOD takes a creative and more reflective approach to Bible reading, with an emphasis on personal renewal.
- ENCOUNTER WITH GOD is for the more experienced Bible reader, providing a thought-provoking, in-depth approach.

SU also produces Bible notes for children, teens and young adults. Do ask for details.

To ask about Bible reading:
- phone our mail order line: 0845 070 6006
- email info@scriptureunion.org.uk
- log onto www.scriptureunion.org.uk
- write to SU Mail Order, PO Box 5148, Milton Keynes MLO, MK2 2YX, UK

SCRIPTURE UNION
USING THE BIBLE TO INSPIRE CHILDREN, YOUNG PEOPLE AND ADULTS TO KNOW GOD